Mosi, my original inspiration, whose loving energy and effervescence continue to infuse our work, innovations and decisions at The Honest Kitchen. With sparkling eyes, giant personality – always the flirt and ever my friend. Until we meet again.

I am very grateful to Rachel and Natalie at RKPR for all their support, dedication and hard work in editing and helping to fine-tune this book, which probably would have been a pamphlet had it not been for their encouragement.

Thanks also to Jen Cadam Design for help with layout and design – and to my team at The Honest Kitchen for allowing me the quiet time needed to work on this project – a labor of love – and for helping to produce, and evaluate many of the recipes.

Last but not least, many thanks to my husband Charlie, children Thalia and Asha and my dogs Willow, Indy and Taro for their patience, understanding and help with the taste tests.

Participating in the preparation of your pet's meals is a new concept for many people, but once you understand and witness the benefits of serving fresh, healthy, home prepared food that's been created with your own hands – and infused with love and good intent – the habit will likely become a part of your routine. Even if it's just for an occasional treat, the fun of making (and sometimes actually sharing) the food that your animal companion consumes is novel and rewarding for everyone!

At The Honest Kitchen's headquarters in a renovated bread factory in downtown San Diego, we are committed to helping pet guardians become truly involved in their pets' lives. We believe in the empowerment that comes from taking control, making informed decisions and above all, making a real difference in the health and well-being of the animal companions with whom we share life.

Being present or "in the moment," aware, in tune and open-minded about trying new things such as complementary medicine or a new way of eating can begin with something as simple as preparing a meal. Please enjoy these recipes, serve them with love and confidence and take comfort in the knowledge that good food energizes the body and nourishes the soul.

The recipes in this book are coded with symbols (see page 7) so that you can easily determine which are for dogs and cats and which ones you can share with your companions as well. While all the recipes contain real, human-quality foods, the preparation (or in some cases parts used, such as organs or offal) make them unsuitable for people. A few recipes have specific instructions on the preparation of your portion of the meal, and of your pet's portion.

Some recipes incorporate The Honest Kitchen's dehydrated pet foods – however, the majority of the meals simply incorporate foods that you'd find in your own kitchen or are readily available from your local food store.

Lucy.

Lucy Postins
Author and friend of Willow, Indian & Taro –
and in loving memory of Mosi.

introduction

7   key
7   cautions
8   traditional chinese medicine food principles
8   portion size guidelines
9   a word about water
9   where to buy your ingredients
10 getting over the numbers

quick & healthy toppings

13 springtime topper
15 sardine & apricot mush
16 chicken with yam & coconut milk puree
17 cooling summer duck parfait
18 salmon & peach cooler
19 warming buckwheat cream
21 sardine salad
22 a pinch of parsley

wholesome treats

25 antioxidant-rich blueberry mini muffins
27 healthy autumn brownies
28 green Force™ & ham treats
29 dream drops
31 nutty pumpkin rounds
33 a puppalicious doggie birthday cake
34 almond butter poppers
35 holiday noshers
37 liver loaf
39 banana pup-cakes
40 butternut bites
41 chicken & garlic treats
43 gluten-free halloween bonbons
44 pilgrim patties
45 summer savories
47 valentines liver nibbles
49 simple roasted organs
50 turkey & cranberry savories

delicious main meals

53 nourishing fall stew
55 canine quiche
56 creamy sole with summer garden vegetables
57 hearty winter stew
59 healthy fish & sweet potato bake
60 potato, kale and celery root soup
61 coconutty turkey soup
63 simple lamb bake
64 salmon saves the day
65 mix'n match meat stew
67 fruity chicken salad
68 ostrich burgers
69 bison meatballs
70 zucchini, chicken & rice casserole

just for cats

73 prowlmelet
75 feline valentine savories
77 liver cake for cats
78 divine feline scramble

food as medicine

81 fleas
82 diabetes – Keen™
83 diabetes – Verve™
84 sensitive tummies exotic blend
85 sensitive tummies simple bake (or not)
86 flexibility fish medley
87 bone & joint support
88 stress less
89 immune support
90 cancer diets: turkey & yams
91 cancer diets: sardines & sweet potatoes
92 itchy skin fish mush

goodness in the raw

95 beef liver & greens
96 chicken liver puree
97 venison mush
98 turkey medley
99 lamb & garden vegetables
100 mediterranean chicken
101 duck & plums
102 turkey & tropical fruits
103 venison & yams
104 beef & cranberries
105 juicing for pets

key

Most of these recipes can be adapted to suit your or your pet's individual needs or taste preferences. Have fun creating something unique! The following is a list of some people-foods that should NOT be fed to cats and dogs:

Chocolate
Candies, especially with the sweetener Xylitol
Grapes
Raisins
Macadamia nuts
Walnuts
Onions

For a complete list of substances that are toxic to pets, visit the ASPCA Animal Poison Control Center online.

c Suitable for Cats

d Suitable for Dogs

p This recipe is delicious enough to be shared by people!

cautions

Most pets adapt very well to dietary variety. I do however recommend that for more sensitive pets or those with any underlying health issues, you discuss the idea of serving home-made meals with your vet, first. Some foods are not suitable for certain medical conditions so it's important to adhere to the philosophy of "first do no harm" in nutrition, as with all aspects of managing your pet's heath.

I recommend that you introduce new foods gradually to allow the appropriate gut flora ('good bacteria') to develop in your pet's gastrointestinal tract. If your pet is not used to dietary variety, some patience may be needed in strengthening his digestive system to allow it to tolerate different sorts of food. Pets who have been used to eating a monotonous or homogenous diet may have a weakened system to begin with that may not be able to easily digest new, fresh food.

traditional chinese medicine food principles

According to Traditional Chinese Medicine (TCM), different food ingredients possess different energetic properties that affect health in varying ways. Some foods are warming (Yang) and others are cooling (Yin). Other foods are more neutral.

Warming (Yang) foods are good for pets who are chilly with low vitality.
Cooling (Yin) foods are good for hot pets who seem restless and may suffer from allergies.

When underlying health problems exist, foods can be used therapeutically to help the body help itself. However, a totally Yin or Yang diet is not generally recommended; a balance of different ingredients is more beneficial, but with an emphasis on ingredients that have the desired property.

Many of the recipes in this book use foods that are considered therapeutic in TCM and notes are made throughout the pages regarding the 'energy' of foods used or (where applicable) ingredients that have a specific affinity for an organ or therapeutic application.

As a final caution, please cook any meats or fish that you will be eating. Similarly, don't feed cooked bones to dogs as these can splinter. The choice about whether to feed raw meat to your pet will depend on your comfort level and possibly the advice of your vet.

portion size guidelines

The amount you feed will depend primarily on your individual pet, his or her appetite, activity level, age and general health. Whether you are mixing a home-made recipe with your companion's usual food or making a totally home-prepared meal will also affect the portion size. The guidelines below are just suggestions on the total amount to offer each day, comprised of commercial and/or home-prepared foods.

If you feed twice a day, then each meal would be half the total amount. Try not to get too hung up on serving sizes. Just as in humans, some meals can be larger than others and it's not usually necessary to weigh out a portion. Use your best judgment for the size of your companion, and the following amounts as a rough guide.

For pets 10 to 30 lbs, a daily ration of ½ to 2 cups is appropriate.
For dogs 30 to 60 lbs, daily rations can vary from 2 to 4 cups total.
For dogs 60 to 100 lbs, 4 to 8 cups is a good daily amount.

a word about water

Many of the recipes in the book call for water, to either re-hydrate an Honest Kitchen™ recipe or for some other purpose. Tap water is acceptable to use, but I highly recommend filtered or bottled water if possible. Many municipal drinking water supplies in certain areas of the United States are now fluoridated and a link has been established between fluoridation in tap water and an increase in the incidence of osteosarcoma (bone cancer) in young men in these same geographical areas. It is likely that fluoridated water also increases the risk of osteosarcoma in dogs, especially neutered males. Many companies now offer 'whole house', 'under sink' or 'refrigerator' fluoride filters that remove this substance back out of the water. Your pet's drinking water should also be filtered of fluoride (as well as other contaminants). In our home, we have a fluoride filter on the line that runs to the fridge and a regular contaminant filter within the fridge and we use this supply for all our drinking and cooking needs, including the hydration of our three dogs' meals. Since the benefits of fluoride are very questionable anyway and many dentists believe that only topical fluoride in the form of toothpaste actually offers any protection against cavities, it may be best to avoid fluoridated water for your human family as well.

where to buy your ingredients

If you can, try to buy fresh, local, seasonal produce from a local farmer's market, or even direct from the farm. This reduces your carbon 'paw print' because fewer resources are used to get foreign or non-local foods to your local supermarket, and your food dollars are kept in your local area. As we select foods for ourselves and our animal companions, we shouldn't think we can't make a difference. Each of us can – by buying mindfully and eating sensibly, with respect for the origins of our food, and a conscious move away from products made by big agribusiness and back to real, recognizable ingredients that still possess the nutrients that sun and earth bestowed upon them.

getting over the numbers

As a result of the propaganda put out by some of the giant pet food conglomerates, many people have become afraid to prepare their pets meals for themselves because they are too nervous about achieving proper nutritional balance in the meals they make. While it's true that meals should be balanced and that companion animals do have minimal requirements for a number of vitamins, minerals and amino acids as well as other nutrients, it's also important to maintain some common sense. We humans establish a nutritional balance throughout the week, by consuming different foods in different meals. Some days we may eat more protein and insufficient calcium or a slight excess of vitamin A or C but a lack of B vitamins – but as long as the diet includes a variety of fresh, seasonal, minimally processed foods, we can still maintain great health because we get all the nutrients we need. The same should hold true for our animal companions too.

I'm always amazed when doing nutritional consultations, how many animal guardians have become obsessed with mg per kg or UI per lb of certain vitamins and minerals, and want to know exactly how much of something is in a serving of food. Yet they don't know nearly as much about the percentages or components in their human children's meals.

We humans don't know how many mg of calcium we consumed yesterday, nor do we measure the phosphorus intake in our children's breakfasts. The basic principles of sensible eating – where we respect whole foods as the foundation of life rather than obsessing about one dietary constituent or another – should apply to pets as well as people. Fixating on one nutrient in isolation will not ensure the diet as a whole is safe, nutritious or abundantly healthy. A far more sensible approach is to give our animal companions a varied diet with a good amount of minimally-processed ingredients that together are nutritionally complete over a period of time. When the diet is varied, it isn't as important to be strict about percentages as it would be if you were feeding processed, commercial food every day.

quick & healthy t♥ppings

The recipes in this section are designed as "accompaniments" or toppings for your pet's regular meals. Despite what many pet food manufacturers might lead you to believe, domestic cats and dogs actually benefit greatly from dietary variety and are no more designed to eat one type food for their entire lives than you or I.

Once an animal is used to eating different sorts of foods, the variety will actually work to strengthen the system. When we feed an abundance of highly processed calories (such as with kibbled food), the body does not have to "work" hard to extract the nutrients. Yes, the body has an innate "desire" to work in order to keep healthy and "tuned up." Without the "work" of processing and digesting real, minimally-processed whole foods, the "fire in the belly" is lost and the body eventually becomes weak. Real whole foods help keep the body healthy by providing this necessary "work" as well as providing more abundant nutrients.

While healthy toppings are not a quick-fix for most health problems, they can help an animal by providing extra nutrients that he or she might not receive in the usual processed food. If you feed low-grade food that's laden with fillers, by-products and hard-to-digest proteins, it will be difficult for your pet to feel any improvement because the culprits of his poor health are still being ingested at each meal. Try to feed the best quality food you can along with healthy toppings for the best chance of providing a really strong nutritional cornerstone to your pet's health.

springtime topper

This tasty yet light combination of flavors provides a nourishing, healthy addition to your companion's usual meal.

ingredients

¼ cup fresh fennel, finely diced, raw or steamed
¼ cup fava beans, lightly cooked
1 tbsp cherries, pitted and diced
½ cup live culture plain yogurt
1 cup cooked ground meat such as turkey (optional)

what to do

1. Combine all the ingredients gently with a spoon in a large bowl.
2. Add a couple of tablespoons of the mix to each of your pet's usual meals.
3. Refrigerate any leftovers for two to three days in a covered container.

Fennel is bursting with powerful antioxidants such as quercitin and some studies are underway to investigate its possible cancer-fighting properties. It's also a warming herb that is very useful for gas and indigestion.

Fava beans are thermal-neutral. They tonify the spleen, liver, kidneys and pancreas.

Cherries are loaded with antioxidants, and nourish the liver and kidneys.

Apricots contain vitamins A and C, potassium and tryptophan. Nutrients in apricots can help protect the heart and eyes, as well as provide the disease-fighting effects of fiber. The high beta-carotene and lycopene activity of apricots makes them important heart health foods. Powdered spirulina is available from health food stores.

sardine & apricot mush

This recipe is inspired by traditional Chinese medicine, and uses foods that tonify the blood and Qi. The ingredients used in this recipe are neutral in traditional Chinese medicine.

ingredients
¼ cup dried apricots
¼ can pumpkin (not pie mix)
1 can low sodium sardines in oil or water
½ cup cooked millet
½ cup plain, live-culture yogurt
1 tsp powdered spirulina (optional)

what to do
1. Drain the sardines. Combine all ingredients together in a bowl and stir gently until thoroughly mixed.
2. Refrigerate the mixture and add a couple of tablespoons to each of your pet's usual meals until it's all gone!

chicken with yam & coconut milk puree

Use this recipe as a snack or topper, which can be served warm or chilled.

The chicken may be fed raw to healthy pets with strong immune systems. Discuss this with your vet, especially if you are feeding younger pups, pregnant females or elderly pets. Please cook the chicken if you plan to share this recipe with your companion.

ingredients
2 lbs yams, peeled and cut into 1 inch cubes
6 tbsp extra-virgin olive oil
1 can of coconut milk
4 large chicken breasts, diced

what to do
1. Preheat oven to 375°F, and lightly oil the baking dish with olive oil.
2. Add the cubed yams to the baking dish and shake gently to coat them with olive oil.
3. Roast the yams in the oven for 40 minutes, stirring and turning after 20 minutes or so until edges are slightly crisp.
4. Remove from oven and blend the yams and coconut milk (in ½ cup increments) in a food processor until the desired consistency is attained.
5. Cut up the chicken breasts into size-appropriate pieces for your pet and sauté in a pan, if desired.
6. Mix the chicken pieces with the yam and coconut puree.
7. Refrigerate any leftovers and serve a small amount with each meal.

Yams are a great source of complex carbohydrates and fiber, and their sugars are released and absorbed very slowly into the bloodstream. This makes them ideal for helping to control blood sugar levels. In addition, yams are a good source of manganese, a trace mineral that helps with carbohydrate metabolism and is a cofactor in a number of enzymes important in energy production and antioxidant defenses.

cooling summer duck parfait

This recipe is super simple to prepare and uses cooling (Yin) foods making a refreshing treat to beat the summer heat. Be sure to use cooked boneless duck if you plan to share this recipe with your animal companion.

ingredients

2 cups lightly cooked boneless duck or raw duck meat and bones
¼ cup cucumber, diced
¼ cup flaked almonds
½ cups fresh spinach, chopped
¼ cup cottage cheese
3 tbsp honey
2 tbsp olive oil
¼ cup diced papaya
1 sprig fresh parsley to garnish

what to do

1. Combine the first six ingredients in a bowl so they are thoroughly mixed.
2. Spoon into a serving dish or use to top your dog's regular food.
3. Sprinkle the papaya on top and finish with the fresh parsley.
4. Serve this as a healthy topping with your pet's usual meals.

Did you know? A calming grain-free recipe such as this is great for sensitive tummies. In traditional Chinese medicine, duck removes dampness, cucumber clears heat, and almonds strengthen the spleen and stomach.

salmon & peach cooler

This recipe is super simple to prepare and makes a refreshing recipe to beat the summer heat. Be sure to use cooked boneless salmon only.

ingredients

1 cup lightly cooked boneless salmon fillet with skin
2 diced fresh peaches, pits removed
¼ cup cucumber, diced
¼ cup flaked almonds
½ cup plain yogurt
3 tbsp honey (optional)
2 tbsp olive oil
1 sprig fresh basil to garnish

what to do

1. Combine the first six ingredients in a bowl so they are thoroughly mixed.
2. Spoon into a serving dish as a snack between meals or use to top your dog's regular food.
3. If you plan to share this recipe, you could serve your portion with some crusty French bread and a glass of chilled chardonnay (optional).

warming buckwheat cream

You should be able to find buckwheat at a health food store. Buckwheat comes in many forms: kasha, kasha grits, whole buckwheat and buckwheat flour.

ingredients
1 cup buckwheat flour
2 tbsp olive oil
4 cups filtered water

what to do
1. Add the oil to a skillet over a low flame and add flour to brown.
2. Stir continuously with a wooden spoon (being careful not to allow it to burn).
3. Once the flour is brown, turn off the heat and allow it to cool slightly.
4. Add the water to the flour and heat it over a high flame until it starts to boil.
5. Lower the heat and simmer, covered, for 15- 20 minutes. Stir occasionally to prevent sticking.
6. Cool the cooked buckwheat to room temperature and serve with your dog's usual meal.

This recipe makes a great breakfast for people, too!

Did you know? Despite its deceiving name, buckwheat is grain-free and gluten-free. While many people think that buckwheat is a cereal grain it's not a wheat or even a grain at all! Buckwheat is actually a fruit seed that is related to rhubarb and sorrel making it a suitable substitute for grains for pets who are sensitive to wheat or other grains that contain protein glutens. It is known for its warming, Yang properties and may be a welcome addition to your pet's winter meal. You may like to season your portion with a little salt if you'll be sharing!

sardine salad

This recipe is perfect to serve as a healthy topper to any type of pet food. Sardines are a great source of essential fatty acids.

ingredients

1 can low sodium sardines* in water or oil
¼ cup fresh green beans, lightly cooked and diced
¼ cup melon (such as cantaloupe), diced finely
¼ cup plain cottage cheese
Dash of cayenne pepper (optional)

what to do

1. Gently combine all the ingredients in a large mixing bowl.
2. Store in an airtight container in the refrigerator.
3. Add the mixture to your pet's food in portions appropriate for his or her size.

*Canned salmon may be substituted for sardines in this recipe, if desired.

Green beans are especially delicious in the warm summer months. They are laden with vitamins and other nutrients that support cardiac and intestinal health, as well as strong bones. They also offer wonderful, natural anti-inflammatory properties. I always recommend fresh, local produce where available but frozen green beans are fine as well.

a pinch of parsley

Parsley is very delicate, so don't use too much heat or you will denature some of its wonderful benefits. If possible, choose vegetables that are in season (your local farmer's market is a great place to look) because Mother Nature provides foods that contain necessary nutrients to support our bodies at certain times of the year.

ingredients
1 cup of fresh garden vegetables of your choice (NO onions)
2 sweet potatoes, sliced and washed (peels on)
1½ quarts water
½ cup fresh parsley, chopped
2 tbsp butter (optional)

what to do
1. Add the vegetables to a pot of boiling water, simmer until soft and remove from the burner.
2. Add the parsley.
3. Mash up any larger pieces of vegetable if you have a small dog.
4. Add a few vegetables, plus the broth to the regular food and sprinkle the parsley on top.

Did you know? Like most fresh garden herbs, parsley possesses powerful health benefits. Parsley's volatile oils have been shown to inhibit tumor formation, particularly in the lungs. This popular herb also contains a mega-dose of vitamin K. Parsley is also recommended by some holistic vets to help combat bad breath and gas!

wh♥lesome treats

This section contains a variety of make-at-home treats that your cat or dog will devour! Since so many commercial pet treats are laden with preservatives, salt, sugar and artificial flavorings, home-made treats are a healthier, more wholesome option. Most of the treats here can be formed to a size that's appropriate for your animal companion. If you're going to use the recipe to make training treats, simply form tiny, bite-sized pieces rather than larger meatballs or cut-out shapes; otherwise your pet will get too full on too few treats and lose some of the motivation to perform!

The preparation time on many of these recipes is extremely quick too! Home-made treats are also a fantastic gift for your pet's special friends. Puppy birthday parties and other 'pets welcome' events are ideal venues to show off your cooking skills and make every pet wish you were his parent!

As noted under each recipe, these treats can all be stored in a refrigerator or frozen, to keep for later. It's important to make sure each recipe is completely cooked before sealing in an airtight container; otherwise they will generate too much moisture which will cause them to spoil. You can make most of the treats even crispier by leaving them in the oven after cooking – just turn off the heat but keep the door closed for two to four hours. This will remove even more of the moisture. Treats that have been frozen should be defrosted in the fridge in quantities that will last a few days.

antioxidant-rich blueberry mini muffins

This recipe is fun to make and tastes delicious. It's a real departure from more usual dog treats! Each of the ingredients here is laden with antioxidants or other important nutrients that support the immune system, especially during stress, chronic illness or aging. You will need a small size muffin pan and small paper cups for this recipe.

ingredients

¼ cup flax meal (or milled flax)
½ cup dried or fresh blueberries
¼ cup wheat germ
¼ cup nutritional yeast
1 tablespoon kelp powder
1 teaspoon vitamin C powder (optional)
2 large free range eggs
¼ cup plain yogurt
1 tablespoon olive oil

what to do

1. Preheat the oven to 350°F.
2. Combine all the dry ingredients including the blueberries (the first six items in the list) in a mixing bowl and fold together to combine thoroughly.
3. Add in the moist ingredients (the last three on the list) and stir again to form a thick batter.
4. Pour this batter into mini muffin pans with paper cups so that they are about half full.
5. Bake for about 25 minutes at 350°F until firm to touch.
6. Cool thoroughly before serving and store in an airtight refrigerator for up to a week.
7. The muffins can also be frozen, if desired.

Did you know? According to the USDA Human Nutrition Research Center on Aging (Boston, MA), blueberries are among the fruits with the highest antioxidant activity. Blueberries have also been found to slow down age-related loss of memory as well as helping to prevent bladder infections, just like cranberries.

healthy autumn brownies

These rich but wholesome brownie-style treats make use of some of fall's healthiest vegetables and fruits. Squash or unsweetened canned yams may be substituted for sweet potatoes, if desired.

ingredients
2 cups of The Honest Kitchen Force™ dehydrated dog food
2 free range eggs
½ cup sweet potato, cooked and mashed
½ cup of cooked parsnips, finely diced
¾ cup of diced ham
¼ cup grated gruyere cheese
¼ cup of dried cranberries
4 tbsp unsweetened applesauce
1½ cups warm meat broth (low sodium, if commercial)
1 small pinch fresh or dried rosemary (optional)

what to do
1. Hydrate the Force™ using the warm meat broth.
2. Crack the eggs into a bowl and whisk lightly.
3. Mix in the applesauce, ham and cheese.
4. Mix the sweet potato (or yam/squash) into the hydrated food, along with the parsnips, cranberries and eggs.
5. Spread in a thin layer onto a well greased baking sheet.
6. Grate a little extra cheese on top, if desired and cook at 300°F for about 60 minutes or until the top is slightly dried and slightly crispy.
7. Cool thoroughly and cut into squares to serve.

Did you know? There is actually a difference between rosemary the plant and rosemary essential oil. The quote below is from Greg and Mary Tilford, master herbalists and authors of the wonderful book "Herbs for Pets."

"The essential oil of rosemary, which represents a concentrated form of a select number of chemical constituents of the plant, is a very different medicine than the whole plant, or a preparation of the whole plant. In other words, where rosemary essential oil represents only a few parts of rosemary's chemistry, rosemary tincture or tea represents hundreds of parts of its chemistry. From an herbalist's perspective the essential oil is closer to being a drug than an herbal medicine. The 'whole plant' is always greater than the sum of its parts. The oil is contraindicated for animals who have any type of seizure disorder."

green force™ & ham treats

These baked treats are quite healthy and super easy to make.

ingredients
⅓ cup The Honest Kitchen Force™ dehydrated dog food
½ cup hot water
½ cup diced ham
1 free range egg
2 tbsp plain yogurt
2 tbsp canola (or safflower) oil
1 cup whole oat flour or instant oats

what to do
1. Preheat the oven to 400°F.
2. Combine the Force™ and water, mix thoroughly and allow to re-hydrate in a bowl for about 5 minutes.
3. Add all the remaining ingredients and stir well.
4. Refrigerate the batter for 30 minutes for best results.
5. Line a baking sheet with parchment paper and drop spoon-sized dollops about 1 inch apart or squeeze 'balls' from a pastry bag.
6. Bake for about 7 minutes at 400° degrees, then to crisp up, turn off the oven and leave the cookies inside for up to 1 hour (dependent on the level of crispness you want, and your oven).
7. Cool before serving.
8. These treats will store in an airtight container in the refrigerator for a week, or freeze for 3 months.

Did you know? Oats are strictly gluten-free. Oats are now on the list of safe foods for people with Celiac disease, or true gluten intolerance. Although dogs (except for Irish Setters) don't appear to suffer from Celiac disease, many do show lower-grade sensitivities to glutenous grains, evidenced by itchy skin, chronic ear infections, GI upset and chewing at the feet, among other things.

dream drops

These tasty treats are incredibly easy to make and taste delicious! You can substitute another type of cheese for the cheddar if you wish, or even use cottage cheese and reduce the water slightly.

ingredients

1 cup The Honest Kitchen Thrive™ dehydrated dog food
¼ cup ham, diced
3 tbsp sharp cheddar cheese
1 free range egg, lightly beaten
1 cup warm filtered water

what to do

1. Preheat the oven to 350°F.
2. Hydrate the Thrive™ with the cup of warm water and stir.
3. Thoroughly mix in the remaining ingredients to form a batter.
4. Spoon the mixture in cherry-sized drops, onto a greased baking sheet and flatten slightly with a teaspoon.
5. Bake in a 350°F oven for 20 minutes.
6. Serve after cooling completely.
7. Dream Drops can be stored in an airtight container in the fridge.

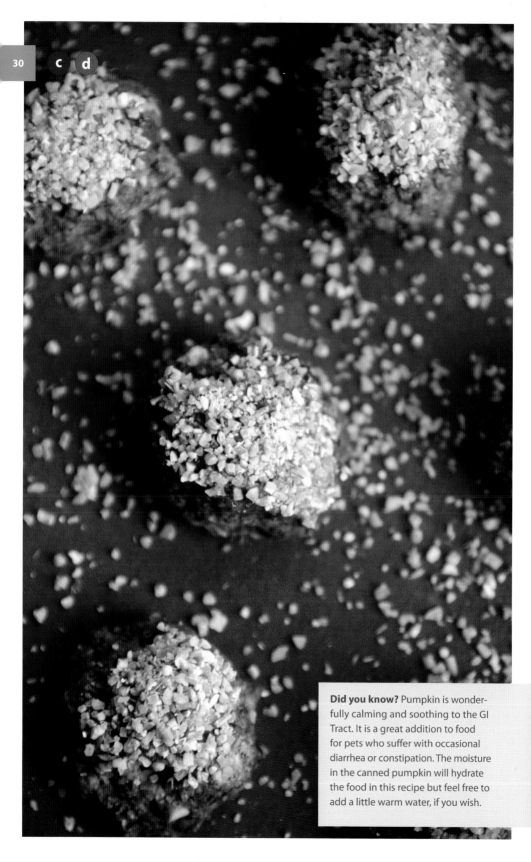

Did you know? Pumpkin is wonderfully calming and soothing to the GI Tract. It is a great addition to food for pets who suffer with occasional diarrhea or constipation. The moisture in the canned pumpkin will hydrate the food in this recipe but feel free to add a little warm water, if you wish.

nutty pumpkin rounds

This recipe was devised by one of our customers, Amanda Johnson from Lakewood CO. Amanda and her husband Bryan are guardians to Dexter, Hanako, Zephyr and QP. Here's the scrumptious recipe she developed, which requires no cooking at all!

ingredients

½ cup canned pumpkin
½ cup almond butter
½ cup The Honest Kitchen Embark™ dehydrated dog food
¼ cup unsalted almonds, finely chopped or flaked for dogs, ground for cats
Carob powder (optional)

what to do

1. In a small bowl mix the pumpkin and almond butter together using a fork.
2. Thoroughly mix in the Embark.™
3. Place in a refrigerator for about an hour until firm.
4. With your hands, roll rounded teaspoonfuls of mixture into balls.
5. Roll the balls in almonds or carob powder, coating them evenly (optional).
6. Place on a cookie sheet in the freezer.
7. When the balls are completely frozen, pack them into airtight containers and store them back in the freezer to defrost and use as needed.

Amanda states, "The plus is that the treat is grain-free, egg-free, and peanut-free (with the use of the almond butter) so all my fur kids can eat them!"

Take care to supervise puppy parties carefully! Monitor portions, supervise to avoid food squabbles and be especially cautious if you do use candles on the cake.

a puppalicious doggie birthday cake

Puppy got a birthday coming soon? This scrumptious (but not too naughty) cake will be sure to make it a special day!

ingredients

cake

4 cups The Honest Kitchen Force™ dehydrated dog food
2 tablespoons The Honest Kitchen Ice Pups™ frozen treat mix
1 cup of chicken stock
2 free range eggs
3 tablespoons honey
1 cup plain yogurt
½ cup smashed up The Honest Kitchen Smooches™ or Nuzzles™ cookies

icing

1 cup plain yogurt
2 strips bacon

what to do

1. Preheat your oven to 350°F.
2. Grease a 10 inch cake pan (you can use butter or vegetable oil).
3. You can also line the pan with a strip of wax paper to encourage easy release.
4. Combine in a bowl the Force™ and the Ice Pups™ and sift together.
5. In a separate bowl, combine the eggs and the yogurt.
6. Whisk at high speed for 3 minutes. Gradually add in honey.
7. Reduce the speed to low and add in the dry mixture cup by cup.
8. Stir in the smashed up cookies.
9. Bake in the oven for 25-35 minutes, until you can insert a toothpick and it comes out clean.
10. Allow the cake to cool on a rack for 10 minutes.
11. Cook the two pieces of bacon and chop them into small pieces.
12. Carefully invert the cake onto a serving dish.
13. Ice with the plain yogurt, sprinkle with bacon bits and serve.

almond butter poppers

These treats are slightly richer than some in the book but that makes them extra special and ideal for important occasions like puppy parties.

ingredients

1 cup almond butter

1 cup milk

1 cup oat flour (sifted) or 1 cup instant oats

1 cup ground beef, cooked

1 cup The Honest Kitchen Verve™ dehydrated dog food

½ cup warm water

2 tsp ground flax seed meal

¼ cup plain yogurt

½ cup dried cranberries

what to do

1. Preheat the oven to 350°F.
2. To make the dough, mix the almond butter, milk, oat flour, and ground flax seeds in a bowl.
3. In a separate bowl, mix Verve™ with warm water and allow to re-hydrate.
4. Combine the two and knead until soft and lubricated.
5. Flatten out the dough to be cut with cookie cutters or roll into small balls (poppers).
6. Bake cookies at 350°F for 15-20 minutes until firm to touch.
7. For the topping, mix the yogurt and cranberries together and stir well.
8. Pour this mixture onto the cookies and spread with a knife after they have been baked.

Did you know? Flaxseed is an excellent source of omega fatty acids and lignans, which are vital for a healthy immune system, heart function and a lustrous coat.

holiday noshers

These unusual fruity, chewy treats make a great gift for your pup's friends if you're visiting for the holidays. This recipe makes a large batch, so there's plenty to share or save for later!

ingredients

½ cup unsweetened applesauce

1 free range egg

½ cup almond butter or coconut oil

1 tsp vanilla essence (optional)

1 cup warm water

½ cup The Honest Kitchen Thrive™ dehydrated dog food

1 cup oat flour

¼ cup dried blueberries

what to do

1. Preheat the oven to 350°F.
2. In a large mixing bowl, combine the applesauce, egg, almond butter, vanilla (if using) and water. In a second bowl, combine the oats, Thrive™ and blueberries.
3. Add the dry ingredients to the wet and mix well.
4. Turn the dough out onto a floured surface and knead until thoroughly mixed together.
5. Roll out the dough to ¼ inch thick and cut out shapes.
6. Place these onto a greased baking sheet and bake for 45 minutes.
7. Cool on a rack before serving.
8. Store in a sealed container in the refrigerator for up to a week, or freeze.

Blueberries are laden with antioxidants and are especially supportive for the eyes. Almonds and almond butter contain significant amounts of protein, calcium, fiber, magnesium, folic acid, potassium, and vitamin E. You can also use coconut oil in place of almond butter for this recipe. There are numerous reports of dogs becoming lean and energetic soon after the addition of coconut oil to their diets. Coconut oil is also excellent for the skin and coat. Problems involving itchy skin, cuts, wounds, and ear problems also are helped, with increased recovery times. Dogs with allergies or contact dermatitis have shown improvements soon after having coconut added to their food.

Pureeing the liver is not for the faint of heart and it may help to look away in the initial stage at least, but it only takes a few seconds and the semi-liquid (if slightly pungent) result blends really well with the other ingredients!

liver loaf

This delicious recipe can be sliced up into any size to make training treats suitable for your individual pet. The added bonus is that this treat is completely grain-free.

ingredients

2 cups fresh raw organic beef liver
2 free range eggs
¼ cup canola or other vegetable oil
1 clove fresh garlic, crushed
2 cups instant oats
1 tbsp applesauce
2 tbsp nutritional yeast (optional)
3 tbsp powdered kelp (optional)
¼ cup flaxseed meal
Filtered water sufficient to make a batter

what to do

1. Preheat the oven to 350°F.
2. Process the liver in a blender or food processor until completely pureed.
3. Beat the eggs in a bowl and pour in the oil.
4. Add the liver.
5. Mix in the dry ingredients slowly, stirring continuously so they are thoroughly combined. Add water gradually, until you have a 'batter' consistency.
6. Pour this batter into a loaf tin.
7. Bake at 350 degrees for 50 minutes.
8. Cool in the tin until able to be handled, then gently turn the loaf out onto a rack and refrigerate to cool completely.
9. Slice with a sharp knife and then dice into bite-sized pieces appropriate for your pet.

banana pup-cakes

This recipe was created by Jenna Hill, The Honest Kitchen's customer service director and baker extraordinaire! Jenna's Boston Terriers, Texi and Roxi, were the willing taste-testers!

ingredients

3 cups The Honest Kitchen Embark™ dehydrated dog food
½ cup almond meal
¼ cup sesame seeds (optional)
2 free range eggs
1 cup warm water
2 tbsp honey, agave nectar or molasses
2 ripe bananas, mashed
½ cup plain yogurt or cottage cheese for topping (optional)
1 extra banana, sliced for topping (optional)

what to do

1. Preheat oven to 375°F. Pre-grease a muffin pan (you can use butter or vegetable oil).
2. Combine the Embark™ and almond meal together in a large mixing bowl.
3. Mix in the sesame seeds if using.
4. Stir in the eggs and then gradually add the honey (agave or molasses) and water.
5. Fold in the chopped bananas.
6. Bake in the oven for about 25 minutes, until you can insert a toothpick and it comes out clean.
7. Let cool on a rack for 10 minutes.
8. Top with plain yogurt or cottage cheese and some sliced bananas on top, if you'd like.
9. Serve them up – and feel ever so popular!

Did you know? Bananas have long been recognized for their antacid effects and their ability to protect against stomach ulcers and ulcer damage. Substances in bananas help activate the cells that compose the stomach lining, so they produce a thicker protective mucus barrier against stomach acids. Bananas also contain substances called protease inhibitors which help eliminate bacteria in the stomach that may be a primary cause of stomach ulcers.

butternut bites

These goodies are easy to make and taste delicious! The cranberries also make them well suited to pets who are prone to urinary tract infections.

ingredients

1 cup boiled and mashed butternut squash (You could substitute mashed pumpkin or sweet potatoes if you don't have butternut squash available.)
1½ cup uncooked oatmeal
¼ cup dried cranberries
1 tsp nutritional yeast
1 tbsp honey

what to do

1. Preheat the over to 370°F and butter a large cookie sheet.
2. Combine the cooked, mashed butternut squash with the oatmeal, cranberries, yeast and honey.
3. Mix well so that all the ingredients are very thoroughly combined.
4. Using a teaspoon, scoop small balls on to the buttered cookie sheet.
5. Make sure they are evenly spaced out about 1 inch apart and bake for about 10 to 12 minutes.
6. Allow the bites to cool, and then add these nutritious goodies to your dog's usual meal or serve them as individual treats!

If your pet suffers from urinary tract crystals, natural supplements can help. First, it's important to determine what type of crystals are present, because most urinary-support supplements act in part by changing the pH of the urine and choosing the incorrect supplement could exacerbate the problem. Your vet should be able to determine the type of crystals and any pH imbalance with a simple test. Struvite crystals (which form when the urine is too alkaline) and calcium oxalate crystals (which form when the urine is too acidic) are the most common types. A natural diet that is high in natural moisture content is especially important too.

chicken & garlic treats

These fun summer treats are also functional, since they contain ingredients thought to naturally help to repel flies, fleas and other insects.

ingredients

2 cups The Honest Kitchen Thrive™ dehydrated dog food
1 cup warm water
2 cups ground chicken
2 cloves garlic, crushed
¼ cup nutritional or brewer's yeast
2 tbsp powdered kelp
2 free range eggs

what to do

1. Preheat your oven to 350°F.
2. Hydrate the Thrive™ with the warm water.
3. Mix in all remaining ingredients one by one, stirring slowly after each addition.
4. Roll into meatballs appropriately-sized for your pet and bake them on a greased baking sheet in a 350°F oven for about 20 minutes.

Yeast is naturally rich in B vitamins, which boost the immune system, calm the nervous system and help to repel fleas, too. Garlic also acts as natural flea repellent. Kelp helps to boost immunity which increases resistance to parasites.

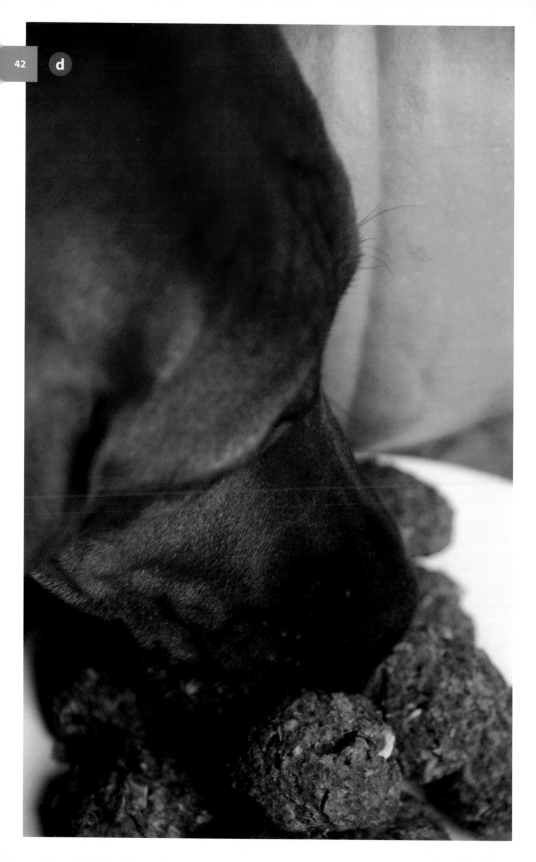

gluten-free halloween bonbons

These treats are quick and easy to make and are suitable for most sensitive pets. Quinoa and buckwheat are not true grains and are very well tolerated even by grain-allergic pets.

Note: Quinoa flour has quite a strong taste and aroma which most pets love but some animals take awhile to get used to it. If you have a fussy pup, buckwheat flour is a perfectly good alternative.

ingredients
1 cup The Honest Kitchen Force™ dehydrated dog food
½ cup ground beef
1 cup canned or fresh cooked pumpkin
1 free range egg
1 small handful of quinoa or buckwheat flour

what to do
1. Preheat the oven to 350°F.
2. Mix equal parts of the Force™ and pumpkin together in a medium sized mixing bowl. Add in the beef, quinoa flour and egg, and mix until well blended.
3. Shape into balls of a size appropriate for your dog, and place it on a greased cookie sheet.
4. Bake for approximately 15-20 minutes or until slightly golden on the outside, but soft in the middle.
5. Cool, and then call in the hounds.
6. These treats will store for about a week in an airtight container in the refrigerator.

Don't forget! Even though Halloween is great fun for humans, it can be a frightening and potentially dangerous time for pets. Trick-or-treating is not a good activity for most pets since they may become frightened by unusual sights and sounds. Make sure your pet is secured before answering the door in case they take fright and try to escape, and be especially careful that they don't have an opportunity to raid the Halloween candy. Chocolate and candies (containing the sweetener Xylitol in particular) can be fatal.

pilgrim patties

These tender patties are perfect for Thanksgiving with their seasonal ingredients, but can of course be made at any time of year!

ingredients

½ cup The Honest Kitchen Embark™ dehydrated dog food
½ cup ground raw turkey
½ cup unsweetened canned or fresh cooked pumpkin
¼ cup dried cranberries
2 free range eggs
2 tbsp canola or safflower oil
2 tbsp fresh parsley
½ cup warm filtered water

what to do

1. Preheat the oven to 370°F.
2. In a large mixing bowl, combine the Embark™ and water.
3. Allow to sit for 5 minutes to re-hydrate sufficiently.
4. Gently fold in the pumpkin, cranberries, oil and parsley.
5. Beat the eggs in a separate cup and stir in.
6. Fold everything together to form a stiff batter.
7. Use two tablespoons (or your hands) to form golf ball-sized shapes.
8. Place these on a large greased baking sheet about 2 inches apart and gently flatten them into thick patties using the back of one of your spoons, or your palm and bake for about 45 minutes.
9. Cool on a rack before serving.
10. These patties can be stored in a sealed container for up to a week.

Pumpkin is bursting with nutrients. It contains lots of vitamin A, an antioxidant vitamin, as well as potassium, and iron for blood function. If you don't have an immediate use for the rest of the pumpkin in the can, you can freeze it in ice cube trays and serve as a frozen treat, or mix it with a little cooked ground meat and stuff into Kongs, which you can freeze and serve later – great to keep your dog busy if she needs to be crated during the Thanksgiving celebrations!

summer savories

These savory treats are unbelievably simple to prepare. They taste so good, your pup will feel like a prince or princess and no one will guess they only took a few moments to make!

ingredients
2 cups The Honest Kitchen Keen™ dehydrated dog food
2 cups warm water
½ cup grated parmesan cheese
½ cup ground beef
¼ cup grated raw zucchini
2 free range eggs

what to do
1. Preheat the oven to 350°F and grease a large baking sheet.
2. Hydrate the Keen™ with the warm water in a large mixing bowl and stir thoroughly.
3. Add in the remaining ingredients to form a thick "batter."
4. Carefully mold the batter into marble-size balls using two teaspoons or your hands.
5. Place the balls on a greased baking sheet.
6. Bake at 350°F for about 25 minutes or until slightly crispy on the outside.
7. Cool thoroughly before serving.
8. You can store Summer Savories in the refrigerator for up to a week.

Zucchini are rich in antioxidants like vitamin C and beta-carotene, as well as calcium and folic acid. They are also a good source of fiber and very well tolerated even by sensitive pets. Zucchini has natural anti-inflammatory properties and 'cold' according to TCM principles.

valentines liver nibbles

This recipe uses heart-shaped or other cookie cutters to make pretty treats as a gift for your pet – or his or her boyfriends and girlfriends – for Valentine's Day or other special occasions.

ingredients

2 cups fresh raw chicken liver, preferably organic
2 free range eggs
2 tbsp olive oil
2 cups instant quinoa flakes
3 tbsp unsweetened applesauce
¼ cup dried cranberries or blueberries
1 clove fresh garlic, crushed
1 tsp of dried basil
Filtered water sufficient to make a batter

what to do

1. Preheat the oven to 350°F
2. Process the liver in a blender or food processor until completely pureed.
3. Beat the eggs in a bowl and pour in the oil.
4. Add the pureed liver.
5. Mix in the dry ingredients slowly, stirring continuously so they are thoroughly combined. Add water gradually until you have a 'batter' consistency.
6. Pour this batter into a flat 1½ to 2" cake tin.
7. Bake at 350°F for 50 minutes.
8. Cool in the tin until able to be handled, then gently turn the 'cake' out onto a rack and refrigerate to cool completely.
9. Use heart-shaped or other cookie cutters to gently press out individual shapes.

If you don't have a cookie cutter, it's also perfectly fine just to cut the loaf into bite-sized squares. Really tiny squares are excellent as training treats because they have a good aroma and can be consumed quickly without filling up your dog's tummy.

The other advantage of cooling this recipe in the refrigerator is that it reduces the risk of thievery by your dog before you have actually finished making it. This is a frequent occurrence with the dogs in our office.

simple roasted organs

This dish can actually double up as a treat or healthy topping to your pet's usual meal. Chicken giblets (hearts, livers and kidneys) are available from butcher shops and many natural food markets. This recipe is super simple and just about all pets love it! Since this recipe is cooked, chicken necks should not be used.

ingredients

4 cups chicken organs/giblets (also called gizzards)
6 tbsp olive oil (organic if possible)
½ tsp dried or fresh rosemary
1 clove garlic, crushed or finely diced

what to do

1. Preheat the oven to 350°F.
2. Arrange the organs in a large roasting pan.
3. Slowly pour on the olive oil and gently shake the pan so that the oil is evenly distributed and thoroughly coats the organs.
4. Sprinkle on the rosemary and crushed garlic.
5. Place in the oven and cook for about 25 minutes, until golden brown and glistening with the oil.
6. Cool thoroughly before serving and refrigerate any leftovers for up to three days.
7. For cats, you can dice the organs finely with a sharp knife before serving.
8. This technique also works well to create bite-sized training treats that are a little bit different.

You can cut the organs into smaller pieces using a sharp knife if you have a very small dog or cat, or one with dental issues.

turkey & cranberry savories

These bite-sized treats are perfect to make your pet feel special during the holidays.

ingredients

2 cups The Honest Kitchen Keen™ dehydrated dog food
2 cups warm filtered water
1 cup raw ground turkey
½ cup grated cheddar cheese
½ cup cooked, mashed sweet potatoes
¼ cup frozen or fresh green beans, finely chopped
¼ cup dried cranberries
2 free range eggs

what to do

1. Heat the oven to 350°F.
2. Mix the Keen™ with the hot water and stir thoroughly.
3. Set it aside to re-hydrate. In another bowl, combine all the remaining ingredients with a wooden spoon and then add in the hydrated Keen.™
4. Use two teaspoons (or your hands) to shape marble-sized dollops and place them on a greased baking sheet.
5. Bake for 20 minutes until the treats are slightly crispy on the outside (check them carefully).
6. Then turn off the oven leaving the treats inside for up to 2 hours.
7. This will enable them to dry out and become crispier.
8. Serve when they are thoroughly cooled, and store in a fridge for up to a week.

While it's lovely to spoil you animal companion with a special meal or home-made treats during the holidays, take care not to over-indulge. Very fatty foods and excessive gorging have been linked to an increase risk of pancreatitis. If you can, just have one family member be responsible for feeding your dog table scraps or other goodies during the holidays so that intake can be monitored – and be sure that any guests are aware that he or she must not be offered any cooked bone at all.

delici♡us
main meals

The recipes in this section are mainly intended as stand-alone diets. They can, however, be offered in smaller amounts as a substitution for just part of your pet's usual meal. If your animal companion isn't yet used to a varied or home-made diet, I recommend going slowly to start off with, and just offer a small amount of your home-prepared food along with his or her regular meal. This will allow the gut flora to adjust to the new food and reduce the chance of digestive disturbance.

Remember, you don't have to prepare home-made food for every single meal, everyday. It's perfectly fine to feed a good quality commercial food the rest of the time, and do home-made as your schedule permits.

Nutritional balance is something that can be achieved throughout the week, and having one meal that is higher in calcium and another that is rather rich in protein, is not in itself detrimental for healthy pets, provided that a variety is offered over time. Different nutrients should be consumed in 'reasonably' balanced amounts during a period of several days.

Just as small children grow up to eat different foods at each meal without specific attention being paid to the precise grams or milligrams of protein or calcium in a particular serving, cats and dogs can be fed with a very similar approach.

Feed with confidence and allow your pet to consume a varied diet from all of nature's bounty. The only exceptions would be for certain 'special needs' pets who really do need a restricted diet for medical reasons. Discuss nutrition with your veterinarian. If he or she is inclined to only ever recommend one brand of food, it might be wise to seek a consultation with another (preferably holistic) vet who is more open minded and has witnessed the benefits of home-made food on other patients.

nourishing fall stew

This recipe makes use of some of the delicious, healthy root vegetables that are plentiful in autumn. The stew is easy to make (though cooking time does take 2 to 3 hours) and can be shared with your pet if you so desire. Once you smell the delicious aroma, it will be hard to resist!

ingredients
4 cups of beef stew meat
2 tbsp olive oil
2 slices bacon, chopped
1 butternut or other seasonal squash, diced into 1 inch cubes
2 carrots, cut in bite-size pieces
1 turnip, quartered
2 tomatoes, quartered
1 small head of celery, coarsely chopped
3 garlic cloves, crushed and chopped (optional)
Water to cover
1 bay leaf (optional)

what to do
1. Preheat the oven to 350°F.
2. Cut the meat into large cubes (or alternatively ask the butcher to do this for you).
3. In a large frying pan, heat the olive oil, add the bacon and lamb and stir until lightly browned. Add the tomatoes, carrots, squash, turnip, celery, garlic and bay leaves.
4. At this point, you can continue cooking the stew in the pan, or transfer it to a casserole that can go in the oven. Cover the ingredients with water and cook either over a low flame or in the oven at 350°F for 2 hours or more.
5. Serve this mixed right in with (or in place of) your pet's regular food. The longer you cook it, the more tender the meat will be. Enjoy your portion with some hearty country bread and red wine if you'd like.

Garlic can be toxic to dogs, but only if fed in very large amounts. According to the Whole Dog Journal, a healthy dog can tolerate 1 clove per 20 lbs of body weight per day without toxic effects.

This recipe is quite rich and should be served in moderation. Eggs are a cooling, Yin tonic. They are also one of the best sources of vitamin D and contain the highest amounts of lutein and zeazanthin when compared to 35 fruits and vegetables. These caroteinoids can help to reduce the occurrence of cataracts and other eye disorders.

canine quiche

This dish was a huge hit with the office pups who were lucky enough to try it.
You may substitute light cream for the kefir for a tastier human version.

ingredients

1 frozen pie crust
3 cups plain kefir
1 tbsp fresh basil (chopped)
1 tbsp extra virgin olive oil
½ cup shredded fresh spinach
4 free range eggs, lightly beaten
¼ tsp salt
A few grinds of black pepper
⅓ cup of parmesan cheese
¼ cup of ground or diced beef or chicken, finely chopped

what to do

1. Preheat the oven to 400° F.
2. Warm the basil and kefir in a small saucepan over low heat for about 10 minutes and set aside.
3. Heat the oil gently in a medium skillet.
4. Add in the spinach and cook until it until it just begins to stick to the pan, and then turn off the heat.
5. Whisk together the warmed kefir, eggs, salt, pepper and cheese.
6. Add all these to the spinach, stirring gently so that everything is thoroughly combined.
7. Sprinkle the meat onto the bottom of the pie crust and cover with the whisked mixture.
8. Bake on the bottom rack for 15 minutes.
9. Transfer the dish to the middle rack of your oven, turn down the heat and bake for another 30 minutes at 350°F (or until it feels firm on top).

creamy sole with summer garden vegetables

Fish of almost any kind makes a wonderful, healthy addition to your pet's regular food once in a while, and this recipe is unbelievably simple to prepare! Sole is a delicately flavored white fish, and can be substituted with other white fish such as orange roughy or halibut, if preferred.

ingredients

4 fillets raw or cooked sole or other white fish, thoroughly de-boned and roughly chopped
¼ cup grated raw zucchini
¼ cup diced string beans
¼ cup grated raw or lightly steamed carrots
¼ cup plain yogurt or cottage cheese
2 tbsp chopped fresh parsley
2 tbsp unsweetened dried blueberries

what to do

1. Gently combine the first five ingredients in a large mixing bowl so that the yogurt or cottage cheese thoroughly coats the fish and vegetables.
2. Sprinkle the parsley and blueberries on top, to garnish.
3. This meal can be divided into single servings to suit the size of your dog, and may be kept in a refrigerator for up to 2 days.

A change to a simple diet with a more novel protein like fish as well as the elimination of grain can be a great first step in combating hotspots, constant itching, dryness, dry hair and associated problems. In addition, using natural home cleaning products and fragrance-free detergents as well as refraining from spraying anything in your yard for a month or two can help if the problem is a contact allergy.

hearty winter stew

This recipe was a huge hit with all the office pups. Although they patiently awaited its arrival into their bowls, they kept drooling all over the place. Be forewarned, your dog will insist on seconds.

ingredients
6 cups lamb stew meat, cut into 1 inch chunks (or smaller depending on your pup's size)
2 tablespoons all-purpose flour
½ cup The Honest Kitchen Preference™ dehydrated dog food base-mix
1 tsp paprika
3 to 6 tbsp olive oil
4 carrots, peeled and cut into ½ inch-thick slices
1 cloves garlic, crushed
2 cups of low sodium chicken stock
3 cups sweet potato chopped into appropriately sized bites
2 cups kale

what to do
1. Preheat oven to 340° F.
2. Pat the lamb dry with paper towels and place in a large bowl.
3. In a shallow bowl, combine the flour and Preference.™
4. Sprinkle the mixture evenly over the lamb and toss well.
5. Heat 3 tablespoons of olive oil in a heavy casserole dish over medium heat.
6. Brown the lamb in batches, adding more oil as needed.
7. When all the lamb is browned, remove it and set aside.
8. Add the carrots and garlic and cook, stirring occasionally, until the vegetables begin to soften; about 10 minutes.
9. Return the lamb to the casserole dish and add in the chicken stock.
10. Bring to a simmer and then add paprika and sweet potatoes.
11. Cover, and place on the bottom rack of the oven at 340°F. Cook until the lamb is very tender, which will take about 2 hours.
12. Pull the stew out of the oven, add in the kale and mix thoroughly so the kale is submerged in the juices.
13. Replace the lid and return to the oven for 10 more minutes.
14. Allow the stew to cool sufficiently before serving in portions appropriate for your dog.

Although higher in saturated fat, lamb is a very good source of protein. Lamb is also a good source of zinc, a mineral that affects many fundamental processes, perhaps the most important of which is immune function.

Oilier fish like mackerel and salmon are richest in essential fatty acids.

White fish like cod and halibut tend to be more suitable for sensitive tummies.

healthy fish & sweet potato bake

This recipe can be made with virtually any sort of fish. Fish is a good choice for pets with skin sensitivities that flare up with more common meats like chicken or lamb.

ingredients

4 fish fillets of your choice, such as salmon or cod

1 large sweet potato, cut into 1 inch cubes (¼ inch for cats)

8 tbsp extra virgin olive oil (canola or other oil may be substituted)

2 heads fresh fennel, chopped

2 cloves garlic, crushed or finely chopped

what to do

1. Preheat the oven to 350°F.
2. Place the sweet potato cubes in a pan of water and boil gently for about 12 minutes until tender.
3. Place the pieces of fish in a 1 inch deep baking pan.
4. Drain the sweet potatoes and carefully arrange the cubes around the fish.
5. Next add the sliced fennel, scattering it evenly around the sweet potato and fish pieces. Add the olive oil liberally and sprinkle on the crushed garlic.
6. Place the pan in the oven and bake for 35 minutes.
7. Allow to cool enough to eat.
8. Your pet's portion may be served alone as an occasional meal replacement, or fed in small portions along with his usual fare.
9. Season your portion with black pepper and sea salt. Mayonnaise and grated parmesan cheese make interesting, optional accompaniments. Serve with a glass of chilled white wine, if desired!

potato, kale & celery root soup

This is a hearty nourishing soup that makes a delicious meal all by itself.
You can also serve it as an accompaniment to your pet's usual food.

ingredients
4 cups celery root, peeled and quartered
5 cups white or Yukon Gold potatoes, peeled and chopped
2 cups chopped kale
1 bay leaf
4 tsp fresh garlic, minced
¼ cup olive oil
2 tbsp of butter
1 cup whole milk
4 cups vegetable or chicken stock

what to do
1. Place potatoes and celery root in stock pot with one pint of water, bay leaf and garlic. Bring to a boil, reduce and simmer until tender.
2. Remove bay leaf and blend in a food processor.
3. Heat olive oil and butter in a stock pot.
4. Add the kale.
5. Sauté until softened and then add the kale to the potato mixture.
6. Add the milk slowly, stirring constantly and then add the stock in small increments to achieve the desired thickness.
7. The consistency should be smooth with the chopped fresh green kale pieces suspended in it.
8. Serve over as an accompaniment to your pet's usual food or as a complete meal.
9. Enjoy with some warm, crusty, buttered bread for yourself.

Kale is a 'leafy green' with beautiful leaves that have an earthy flavor and more nutritional value for fewer calories than almost any other food. It is laden with vitamins A and C, as well as manganese and several other important minerals. Kale is in season from the middle of winter through the beginning of spring when it has a sweeter taste and is more widely available.

coconutty turkey soup

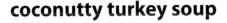

Leftover turkey "scraps" (remember, no cooked bones) can serve as an innovative base for soups like this. This meal is quite rich, so just serve it in small amounts to your dog to make sure he can tolerate it.

ingredients

2 cups turkey stock (or chicken broth may be substituted)
1 cup water
1 to 2 lbs turkey meat, cooked – no bones for this meal
1 cup turkey organ meats, preferably organic
(optional – if you prefer, you can omit if sharing with your pet)
1 cup whole coconut milk (or seven ounces creamed coconut or coconut shavings)
1 tsp fresh grated ginger root
Juice of ½ lemon
1 cup spinach
1 tbsp finely chopped cilantro

what to do

1. Bring the stock to a boil, and simmer gently for about five minutes, skimming off any foam that rises to the top.
2. Slowly add in the coconut milk, lemon juice and ginger, and stir carefully.
3. Simmer on a moderate heat for about 15 minutes.
4. Add the spinach and cooked turkey meat to the pan, and wait for about two minutes to allow these two ingredients to warm up.
5. Ladle the mixture into bowls.
6. Garnish with cilantro and cool slightly before serving.
7. You can store this recipe in an airtight container in the refrigerator for 3 to 4 days.

Did you know? Turkey stock helps with hydration and is a rich source of mucous-thinning amino acids. Organ meats contain vitamin B-1, copper and iron. Coconut is high in fatty acids (lauric acid) and has been shown to have many immune-enhancing properties especially in dogs. Spinach is rich in potassium, vitamin A, vitamin K, beta-carotene and lutein.

simple lamb bake

This bake is extremely easy to prepare and you can actually substitute other ground meats like turkey or beef, for the lamb, if you prefer.

ingredients
2 cups ground raw lamb
1 cup The Honest Kitchen Preference™ dehydrated dog food
1 cup warm water
2 free range eggs
3 cups cooked mashed sweet potato

what to do
1. Preheat the oven to 370°F.
2. Sauté the lamb in a large pan, stirring constantly until it is browned.
3. Combine the Preference™ and water in a mixing bowl and mix thoroughly.
4. Crack the eggs into the Preference™ mix, and stir.
5. Add the lamb to the bowl and stir again.
6. Place the mixture in an oven-proof dish and gently spoon the mashed sweet potato on top so the lamb is completely covered with an even layer.
7. Bake in a 370°F oven for about 40 minutes and cool completely before serving.

Lamb is a fatty, calorie-dense meat that's often recommended for dogs who are slightly lean and need to gain a little weight. Lamb contains considerably more calories and fat than lean hamburger or ground turkey. The natural fat content is also great for the skin and coat.

In addition to the higher fat in meat like lamb, the higher carbohydrates and calories found in sweet potatoes can also help an underweight dog to pack on some extra pounds, when fed long-term.

salmon saves the day

If you plan to share this meal with your animal companion, your portion may be seasoned with a little salt and black pepper. You can also serve your portion with basmati rice or some mashed potatoes and a glass of chilled Pino Grigio (optional).

ingredients

1 large wild boneless salmon filet
1 cup of fresh watercress
½ tsp fresh dill
Olive oil

what to do

1. Pre-heat the oven to 350°F.
2. Place the salmon filet on a baking sheet and drizzle lightly with olive oil.
3. Turn the salmon over and add a little more oil.
4. Bake for about 20 minutes until the flesh is pale but slightly darker in the center.
5. Remove the salmon from the oven and allow to cool.
6. Gently break up the fish flesh into flakes with a fork.
7. Roughly chop the watercress and dill.
8. Combine the greens with the fish in a mixing bowl and add a couple lugs of olive oil.
9. Mix in a small amount with your pet's regular food.
10. This mixture will keep for 2 to 3 days in a covered container, in a refrigerator.

The oils in salmon are especially rich in vital omega-3 essential fatty acids, which are great for combating itchy skin via a natural anti-inflammatory effect. In addition to a grain-free diet, this salmon-based recipe can be fed to cats and dogs to help supply the nutrients they need for healthy skin and shiny hair too.

The Sierra Club recommends always buying wild and not farmed salmon, because wild salmon is more nutritious and does not cause pollution as farmed salmon does. We generally don't recommend feeding totally raw salmon to pets as it can contain a parasite that affects dogs (which is completely harmless after cooking).

mix'n match meat stew

This recipe can be made with just about any sort of meat. If you're lucky enough to have access to exotic meats, such as buffalo or venison, it can make this stew even better.

ingredients

3 cups cubed meat – such as chicken, beef, turkey or other meat of your choice
4 cups of chicken or beef broth (sodium free), warm water may be substituted, if preferred
1 cup fresh chopped vegetables such as:*
1 large carrot
1 medium zucchini
1 head of broccoli
½ small winter squash

what to do

1. Sauté the cubed meat in olive oil for about 10 minutes until browned.
2. Add in the broth and vegetables and bring to a simmer.
3. Cook for about 1½ hours until vegetables are tender.
4. Reserve one portion for yourself.
5. Ladle a size-appropriate serving on to your pet's usual food or serve as a stand alone meal.
6. Your portion would go well with a baked potato, chives and butter, and a glass of Cabernet Sauvignon (optional).

*Never feed onions to dogs!! While usual 'human' stew recipes call for onions, they are toxic for canines and can cause anemia. If you'd really like some onions in your portion, you could slice and sauté these separately in some butter or oil and add to your meal right at the end. Other foods that are toxic – and potentially fatal – to dogs, include chocolate, grapes, raisins and macadamia nuts.

Did you know? Organic, hormone and antibiotic-free meats are best for your pet because they help to reduce the risk of developing antibiotic resistance. If you can find free-range meat, you're supporting a farming method that is kinder and more respectful of the animals who are being raised for food. Always try to buy fresh and local if you can!

Did you know? Yogurt with a live culture is excellent for helping to balance your pet's GI Tract and is especially useful if he or she has to take a course of antibiotics at any time. Apple cider vinegar is thought to act as a natural flea repellent when taken internally.

fruity chicken salad

This recipe is a great way to incorporate some fresh, raw fruit and vegetables into your pet's diet if he usually eats only cooked food.

ingredients

2 cups chicken, cooked* and cut into cubes
¾ cup celery, sliced
¾ cup melon, cubed
¾ cup fresh peaches, peeled and cubed
½ cup plain yogurt or sour cream
1 tbsp apple cider vinegar
1 tbsp pineapple juice
Seasoning salt to taste (for your serving only)

what to do

1. Toss the chicken, celery, melon and peaches together gently.
2. Mix the yogurt or sour cream and other liquids together and pour them over the salad.
3. Mix gently and serve right away, or refrigerate until ready to use.
4. Serve your dogs' portion poured over his usual food.

*If you don't plan on sharing this with your dog, you may use raw chicken rather than cooked. Normal rules about safe food handling and preparation apply.

Don't be tempted to include grapes or raisins in your dog's portion, either. These have the potential to cause kidney failure in dogs.

ostrich burgers

These burgers are fun to make and extremely popular even with the pickiest pets.
You can also use other ground meats, if you can't find Ostrich.

ingredients

1 clove garlic, finely minced
2 tbsp of finely chopped red or green bell pepper (optional)
1 tsp olive oil
1 lb ground ostrich meat
½ tsp freshly ground black pepper
1 tsp salt (optional)

what to do

1. Sauté the peppers (if using) and the garlic in olive oil. Allow to cool slightly. Gently mix the sautéed vegetable mixture with the meat, salt and pepper, combining thoroughly with a wooden spoon. Shape into burgers.
2. Preheat the grill, and then brush the meat with oil and grill for about 4 minutes on each side.
3. Serve your dog or cat's burger broken into size-appropriate pieces with his or her usual meal.
4. Prepare your burger with your choice of sautéed mushrooms, guacamole, onions, sliced tomatoes, and lettuce and serve in a whole grain bun, along with a glass of cold beer (optional).

Exotic meats like ostrich and bison can offer some welcome variety for you and your dog. Switching away from more usual meats also means a slightly different amino acid profile, which can be beneficial for ailing pets.

bison meatballs

You could substitute rabbit, venison or a more common meat for this recipe depending on what you have access to in your local area.

ingredients

2 cups ground lean bison (buffalo) meat

¼ cup bread crumbs (for grain-intolerant pets you can omit this)

¼ cup chopped cilantro or Italian parsley

1 free range egg, beaten

3 ounces crumbled cheese (feta or similar)

½ tsp ground cinnamon

½ tsp black pepper

2 cloves garlic, minced

what to do

1. In medium bowl combine the bison, bread crumbs, cilantro, egg, cheese, olives, salt (optional), cinnamon, black pepper and garlic.
2. Mix until well blended and shape into meatballs that are size-appropriate for your pet and you.
3. To prepare a skewer: Alternate the vegetables and meatballs on skewer.
4. To barbecue: Allow the coals to burn down to an ash grey color.
5. Barbecue the bison and vegetable skewers for 5 minutes, turn, and grill for another 4-5 minutes.

For dogs who are already on a raw meat diet, cooking is optional.

If you share this recipe with your pet, some pasta, fresh salad and cold beer would be good optional accompaniments!

Here's a quick comparison of the health benefits of two exotic and conventional meats.

Ostrich: Fat = 2.80 gm / Calories = 140
Bison: Fat = 2.42 gm / Calories = 143
Beef: Fat = 9.28 gm / Calories = 211
Chicken: Fat = 7.41 gm / Calories = 190

Comparison based on certified independent research Sept. 1991, Feb. 1993 and USDA research revised May 1990. Based on buffalo sirloin, beef sirloin (choice), and chicken breast with skin on. All samples 100 grams (3.5 oz).

zucchini, chicken & rice casserole

This delicious recipe is best for summer time when zucchini and other squash are at their prime. The recipe produces a large batch and you could freeze leftovers in individual portions, if you wish.

ingredients
4 tbsp olive oil
1 cup red bell pepper, chopped (optional)
1 cup carrot, grated
1 garlic clove, minced
3 cups zucchini, diced
3 cups boneless chicken, cooked and diced
1 cup uncooked organic brown rice
2½ cups organic low-sodium chicken broth or water
½ tsp rosemary
½ cup grated parmesan cheese
2 cups chopped tomatoes

what to do
1. Preheat the oven to 350°F.
2. Heat 3 tbsp of the oil in a large pan, and sauté ½ cup of the pepper (if using) and other vegetables and garlic, for about 2 minutes.
3. Add in the cooked chicken, rice, broth, rosemary and the cheese. Mix thoroughly.
4. Place this mixture in a greased medium baking dish.
5. Heat the remaining 1 tbsp oil in skillet, and add the rest of red pepper and tomatoes. Spoon this as a topping, over the rice and chicken mixture.
6. Bake at 350°F for about 1 hour.
7. Serve hot for the humans with a glass of chilled chardonnay (optional).
8. The casserole can be served alone as a complete meal for your dog, or in smaller increments mixed in with their usual food.

Chicken is a very good source of the cancer-protective B vitamin, Niacin. A deficiency of B vitamins has been directly linked to genetic (DNA) damage.

Chicken is also a good source of the trace mineral, selenium, which is vital for overall health. It is an essential component of several major metabolic pathways, including thyroid hormone metabolism, antioxidant defense systems and immune function. A number of studies have suggested a strong inverse correlation between selenium intake and the incidence of cancer.

just f♥r cats

Cats are obligate carnivores and their diet should be made up almost exclusively (or at least predominantly) with meat.

They can tolerate a high amount of fresh protein in their food. Cats are also creatures of habit so it can sometimes be challenging to introduce a more varied diet. They also may be partial to one sort of texture or another, so if you have trouble getting your cat to eat a certain recipe or type of food, try making it either smoother or chunkier in consistency and see if that helps.

Dry, kibbled food is not a healthy choice for cats, who are desert creatures by nature and thus require most of their moisture intake to come from their food. If your cat is a 'kibble addict' you can try gradually phasing in some moist food (either fresh raw meat, home-cooked or even canned meats) to wean him or her over to a diet that's more biologically appropriate for his delicate system. This will help reduce the likelihood of his developing urinary tract and kidney problems later in life.

In the long term, a diet that consists of very low moisture with a biologically inappropriate poor quality protein (by-products) as well as toxic preservatives like BHA, BHT and Ethoxyquin, will tax the kidneys. In a susceptible pet, this can result in impaired renal function, renal disease and true kidney failure – causing severe pain and discomfort for the patient.

Many conventional vets have historically recommended that cats and dogs with kidney disease be fed a diet that is worryingly low in protein. The theory is that these specially formulated 'kidney diets' with their highly restricted protein will be helpful for the kidneys, whose role is to process protein for use by the body. Less protein, the theory goes, will tax the kidneys less. But the fact is that cats and dogs need high protein and despite these low protein kidney diets being fed, no increase in survival rates has been documented.

Dogs and cats with kidney disease need a diet that has moderate protein which is easily digestible. A diet that contains very low protein in the form of by-products like beaks, feet, hair, hides and feathers is actually even more difficult for the kidneys to assimilate than one with more protein in a pure, highly digestible form. Keeping the percentage of meat about the same but using a fattier meat may be helpful as well.

In addition to easy-to-digest protein, a pet with kidney disease also needs sufficient vegetables or other fiber to bind with phosphorus in the digestive tract, and adequate vitamins and minerals. Keeping the pet lean and supplementing with glandular extracts is also helpful and recommended by many holistic vets.

prowlmelet

Cats say it is just delicious! Felines are texture-oriented creatures. So amend this recipe to suit your cat's texture preference by cutting or pureeing the organs to the right consistency and adjusting the cooking time.

ingredients

½ cup The Honest Kitchen Prowl™ dehydrated cat food
½ cup warm water
1 free range egg
1-2 chicken hearts
1 organic chicken liver
½ tbsp dried unsweetened cranberries (optional)

what to do

1. Re-hydrate the Prowl™ with the water.
2. Add in the egg and whisk for about 30 seconds.
3. Lightly sauté the organ meats, if you wish (our office cat, Harry, prefers them raw).
4. Sauté the egg mixture, folding in the raw or cooked organ meat.
5. Cook to your felines' texture preference, add the cranberries if using; cool and serve.
6. Keep any leftovers in an airtight container in the refrigerator and use up within 2 to 3 days.

Eggs are rich in tryptophan, selenium and iodine. They are also a great source of choline, which is a key component of many fat-containing structures in cell membranes, whose flexibility and integrity depend on this nutrient.

The chicken hearts and livers can be chopped roughly or left whole, depending on your cat's desire to chew and gnaw his food.

The process for making kitty-sized treats is a little time-consuming but this recipe makes quite a large batch of treats that can be frozen for several months and defrosted in the fridge a few at a time, so your hard work will last for a while!

feline valentine savories

These bite-sized nibbles are irresistible for most cats and a great way to show your kitty a little extra love on Valentine's Day or any special occasion.

ingredients

1 cup The Honest Kitchen Prowl™ dehydrated cat food

⅓ cup warm water

½ cup grated parmesan cheese

½ cup fresh raw ground turkey

2 free range eggs

what to do

1. Preheat the oven to 350°F.
2. Hydrate the Prowl™ with the warm water in a large mixing bowl and stir thoroughly.
3. Add in all the remaining ingredients one by one and stir to form a thick dough.
4. Carefully mold the dough into small raspberry-sized balls using your hands.
5. Place on a greased baking sheet.
6. Bake at 350°F for about 25 minutes or until slightly crispy on the outside.
7. Cool thoroughly before serving.
8. Keep these treats in an airtight container in the fridge for up to a week or keep them in the freezer and just defrost a few at a time.

C

liver cake for cats

This recipe is nutritious and delicious and can be sliced up very small as a treat or meal topping. The added bonus is that this treat is gluten-free.

ingredients

2 cups organic chicken liver
2 free range eggs
4 tbsp vegetable oil
3 tbsp unsweetened canned pumpkin
1 cup instant oats
2 tbsp nutritional yeast (optional)
Filtered water sufficient to make a batter

what to do

1. Preheat the oven to 350°F.
2. Process the liver in a blender or food processor until completely pureed.
3. This takes a few minutes and it might be best to look the other way as the initial stage is slightly stomach-churning for some people!
4. Beat the eggs in a bowl and pour in the oil.
5. Add liver to egg mixture.
6. Mix in the dry ingredients slowly, stirring continuously so they are thoroughly combined. Add the water gradually, until you have a 'batter' consistency.
7. Pour batter into a loaf or cake pan.
8. Bake at 350°F for about 50 minutes until the cake is firm to the touch on top.
9. Cool until the cake can be handled, then gently turn it out onto a rack and refrigerate to cool completely.
10. Slice with a sharp knife and then dice into bite-sized pieces appropriate for your cat.
11. This recipe can be frozen, if desired. It works well to put small handfuls of the bite-sized pieces into zip-lock bags and freeze them so that you can take out one bag at a time to defrost (then store in a refrigerator) as needed.

Did you know? Pumpkin is great for gastrointestinal health and is wonderful for helping to soothe an occasional tummy upset.

divine feline scramble

This nutritious menu idea will be sure to delight the feline in your life!

ingredients
4 tbsp The Honest Kitchen Prowl™ dehydrated cat food
4 tbsp warm water
1 raw or lightly scrambled free range egg
1 tbsp plain yogurt
4 turkey gizzards, ground or chopped up
½ tsp fresh parsley
1 tsp chopped fresh wheatgrass or dried catnip (optional)

what to do
1. Hydrate the Prowl™ with 4 tbsp of warm water and allow to sit for a few minutes.
2. Beat the egg (cook lightly if desired) and stir into the Prowl.™
3. Pour this mixture over the chicken gizzards.
4. Add the yogurt on top and garnish with a small sprinkle of parsley and the optional ingredients, if you wish.

Gizzards, otherwise known as giblets, include organ meats such as the heart, liver and kidneys, as well as the neck of a turkey or other bird. They are a favorite food of most cats and can be fed raw or lightly cooked except for the neck, which should only be fed raw because it contains bone and cartilage. Since turkey gizzards are rather large, they should be chopped up for this recipe.

f♡od as medicine

Did you know that many foods actually have medicinal benefits?

traditional chinese medicine

Certain ingredients are extremely well suited to particular medical conditions because of Yin or Yang properties or affiliations they have for certain organs or body systems, according to traditional Chinese medicine (TCM) principles – or simply because of their nutritional makeup.

ayurveda

Ayurveda is another approach to medicine, that originates from India. Ayurvedic medicine sets out to treat and prevent disease using a system of fresh whole seasonal foods and spices. Ayurveda recognizes three doshas, or 'elemental types': vata, pitta and kapha. Certain doshas do better with certain types of foods. Some foods aggravate or upset one dosha or another. Ayurvedic medicine is a complex but very interesting approach to health and one that some holistic veterinarians follow as part of their treatment plans.

whole foods

In many cases, food can be 'medicinal' or therapeutic simply because a fresh, whole food diet is being used in place of a heavily processed diet laden with toxic chemicals, fillers, by-products and other harmful substances that slowly deplete general health over time. Fresh real food direct from the earth (or as close to it as possible) is almost without exception, more healthful than food products that have come to your kitchen via big agribusiness or an industrialized food producer.

Food truly is medicine in many ways, and nutrition forms a vital cornerstone to total health. When an underlying medical condition exists, it is of course vital to discuss any planned diet changes with your veterinarian, but it is sometimes possible to reduce medications when the diet is amended appropriately for the problem at hand.

fleas

Fleas can plague our pets in the warmer summer months. They are usually less problematic for healthy pets on a good quality diet, but sometimes additional measures are needed. Rather than dose your pet with harmful pesticides, these treats supply naturally repellent ingredients to help your pets fleas flee.

ingredients
1 cup The Honest Kitchen Verve™ dehydrated dog food
1 cup warm water
2 cups ground beef
2 tbsp powdered kelp or spirulina
2 free range eggs
2 cloves garlic, crushed
¼ cup nutritional yeast (be sure not to use brewers yeast)

what to do
1. Hydrate the Verve™ with the warm water.
2. Mix in the remaining ingredients one by one, stirring slowly after each addition.
3. Serve as a complete meal in an amount that's suitable for your individual pet.

Yeast is naturally rich in B vitamins, which boost the immune system, calm the nervous system and naturally repel fleas, too. If possible, try to avoid using chemical based pesticides on your pet. They are effective, but the side effects are not fully understood and it's likely they have a number of adverse results for our animal companions.

If necessary, an occasional topical flea repellent in the hot summer months is OK if you aren't able to resolve in infestation with natural remedies, but don't use pesticides, or heartworm medications, year round – discuss your pet's needs and the natural alternatives to pesticides, with a good holistic vet. Requirements will depend on your pet's lifestyle and your geographical location.

diabetes

This is a second variation of the diabetes diet, which uses turkey instead of beef, and quinoa in place of the yams. You can use pre-cooked quinoa if you can't find the instant flakes.

ingredients

1 cup The Honest Kitchen Keen™ dehydrated dog food
1½ cups warm filtered water
1 cup raw or lightly cooked ground turkey
½ cup instant quinoa flakes
¼ cup finely chopped green beans, raw or steamed
1 tbsp oil such as flax, safflower or salmon
2 tbsp chopped dandelion greens

what to do

1. Re-hydrate the Keen™ with the warm water in a large mixing bowl and allow to sit for a few minutes.
2. Stir in the turkey and instant quinoa flakes.
3. Add in all the remaining ingredients and combine thoroughly.
4. Store the mixture in a refrigerator for up to three days or freeze in individual portions and serve as needed.
5. Serve the food on a pre-set schedule and portion size established by your veterinarian, to help maintain correct blood sugar levels.

Did you know? It's important to keep diabetic pets on a very regular feeding schedule, and avoid lots of treats between meals. Exercise is also vital, in helping to control diabetes. Make time to go for walks and play with your pet every day! Regular exercise uses energy, which helps to avoid hyperglycemia. Increased blood flow during exercise improves insulin absorption, which helps to further reduce blood glucose levels.

diabetes

Higher fiber is ideal for dogs with diabetes because it can help to regulate the flow of carbohydrates into the bloodstream.

ingredients
1 cup The Honest Kitchen Verve™ dehydrated dog food
1 cup warm filtered water or low sodium chicken broth
1 cup raw or lightly cooked ground beef
½ cup steamed yams, mashed
¼ cup finely chopped green beans, raw or steamed
1 tbsp oil such as flax, safflower or salmon
2 tbsp chopped parsley

what to do
1. Re-hydrate the Verve™ with the warm water in a large mixing bowl and allow to sit for a few minutes.
2. Stir in the beef.
3. Add in all the remaining ingredients and combine thoroughly.
4. Store the mixture in a refrigerator for up to three days or freeze in individual portions and serve as needed.
5. Serve the food on a pre-set schedule and portion size established by your veterinarian, to help maintain correct blood sugar levels.

Did you know? Green beans and oats (found in the Verve™) as well as vegetable sprouts, actually have an insulin-like activity which make them especially useful for diabetes. For cats, a pure meat diet is thought to be helpful for diabetes. Yams are known for their low glycemic index rating, making them well suited for diabetes patients.

sensitive tummies exotic blend

This simple mix of foods is easy to prepare and can be fed as a meal replacement or healthy topping to your companion's usual food. Exotic meats are often the preferred protein source for pets who are intolerant of more common meats.

ingredients

4 cups fresh raw or cooked ground bison, venison or other exotic meat
½ cup cooked mashed sweet potato
¼ cup fresh papaya, finely diced
½ cup plain live-culture yogurt

what to do

1. Combine all the ingredients in a large mixing bowl and store in a refrigerator.
2. Serve as a complete meal, or a little at a time mixed with your pet's regular food.

Did you know? Orange colored fruits and vegetables like papaya and sweet potato are loaded with vitamin A and beta-carotene which are important for a healthy immune system. The enzymes in papaya and the probiotics in live yogurt also support immunity and are especially helpful for gastro-intestinal health.

sensitive tummies simple bake (or not)

This recipe is super-simple for sensitive pets who need an ultra-minimalist diet for a few weeks to help identify dietary allergens. Turkey and sweet potatoes are a top choice among holistic vets. The idea is to feed this 'elimination diet' combination and nothing else, even treats, for 3 to 4 weeks and then gradually add in new ingredients, one at a time every few days, and monitor closely for adverse reactions.

ingredients
3 cups fresh ground turkey
3 cups raw sweet potatoes, sliced with peel on

what to do
Super versatile in nature – you can make this recipe a couple ways:

option 1
1. Lightly sauté the ground turkey until browned and place in a baking dish.
2. Boil the sweet potatoes until soft, and then mash.
3. Add the sweet potatoes in a layer over the turkey.
4. Cool before serving and refrigerate leftovers, to serve a portion at each meal.

option 2
1. Place the raw turkey in a large bowl, cover and refrigerate.
2. Steam the sweet potatoes until softened.
3. Allow the sweet potatoes to cool completely in a refrigerator so that both ingredients are the same temperature in their respective bowls.
4. When thoroughly cold, combine the sweet potatoes with the turkey using a wooden spoon.
5. Serve a portion appropriate for your pet's size, for each meal.

You can store this recipe for 2 to 3 days in a refrigerator. Larger batches can also be produced in one session, and then frozen in individual servings appropriate for your pet. Defrost in the fridge a day or so ahead of time.

Did you know? Slippery Elm is one of the most valuable herbs for GI upset; it soothes and protects and helps to regulate the system. Plantain and fennel are useful to try.

Supplementation with a digestive enzyme can help with numerous chronic digestive disturbances.

For acute conditions such as sudden diarrhea, the homeopathic remedy Arsenicum Album can work wonders. For loss of appetite, a teaspoon of honey, offered alone, may be all that is needed to return things to normal. Ipecacuanha, a homeopathic remedy, is useful for vomiting and nausea.

flexibility fish medley

This is a variation on the prior. You can interchange these two recipes and add either to your pet's usual food if you don't want to feed just this combination alone.

ingredients

1 cup instant oatmeal
1 cup hot water
2 cups cooked wild salmon, carefully de-boned
2 tbsp cold water fish oil
¼ tsp cayenne pepper

what to do

1. Mix the instant oats together in a large bowl.
2. Add in the hot water and stir thoroughly.
3. Add in each of the remaining ingredients one by one and stir.
4. Refrigerate this mixture for up to 3 days and scoop out a size-appropriate serving for your pet as needed.

I don't recommend feeding raw salmon to dogs because it (as well as other anadromous fish) can contain a parasite that is harmful to canines (but rendered harmless during cooking). Cats are able to eat raw salmon without problems.

Arnica, Rhus Tox and Rhuta Grav are three excellent homeopathic remedies to consider for bone and joint discomfort, as well as injuries, sprains and strains. Discuss with your holistic veterinarian or a homeopathic or holistic practitioner to determine what's best for your pet.

bone & joint support

This is a good recipe to serve to aging pets, as well as large breed dogs who may be genetically predisposed to hip dysplasia or other bone and joint woes.

ingredients

1 cup instant quinoa flakes
1 cup hot water
2 cups raw chicken necks and backs, ground to a consistency suitable for your pet
2 tbsp cold water fish oil
2 tbsp dried 'cut and sifted' alfalfa (available from health food and specialty tea stores)
¼ tsp cayenne pepper

what to do

1. Add the quinoa flakes in a large bowl.
2. Add in the hot water and stir thoroughly.
3. Add in each of the remaining ingredients one by one and stir.
4. Refrigerate this mixture for up to 3 days and scoop out a size-appropriate serving for your pet as needed.

stress less

This is a calming recipe that you can serve on an ongoing basis for anxious pets, or occasionally prior to upcoming stressful situations.

ingredients
2 cups ground turkey
1 cup organic oats or millet
1 firm banana, peeled and sliced
1 cup romaine lettuce, finely chopped
1 chamomile tea bag
1 cup of hot filtered water
2 tsp nutritional yeast

what to do
1. Cook the oats or millet according to the package directions.
2. Place the chamomile tea bag into the cup of hot filtered water.
3. Stir gently and then leave for about 4 minutes, to allow the tea to steep.
4. In a large mixing bowl, combine the turkey and the cooked millet or oatmeal.
5. Stir thoroughly and then very gently fold in the banana slices and chopped romaine. Remove the tea bag from the cup and add the tea to the bowl.
6. Sprinkle in the yeast.
7. Serve in portions appropriate for your pet and store any leftovers in the fridge for 2 to 3 days.

Did you know? If your dog suffers from tension or anxiety, you can hydrate his or her food with a warm chamomile tea, rather than plain water, to help calm and relax her prior to stressful events.

For separation anxiety, many dogs respond well to a raw beef marrow bone or Kong™ type toy stuffed with cream cheese or peanut butter, being offered to them as you leave. Their focus will be turned to the treat at hand and you may be able to slip out with minimal upset. Always ensure your dog is offered a raw bone large enough that he cannot choke on it. If your dog is an aggressive chewer or you aren't comfortable leaving him unattended with a bone, the Kong or other interactive treat-dispensing toys are safer options.

Anxiety that arises suddenly from a stressful event can usually be alleviated with a few drops of Rescue Remedy™ directly on the tongue (do not insert the glass dropper right into the mouth, use your fingers to apply to the gums if you are unsure) or behind the ears. Rescue Remedy is also reported to work well for heat exhaustion in the immediate stages, on the way to the vet.

immune support

The ingredients in this recipe provide essential fatty acids, B vitamins and other compounds necessary to support the immune system. A recipe like this is great pre and post-vaccination.

ingredients
2 cups fresh or frozen wild salmon
1 cup wild rice
3 tbsp live culture plain yogurt
1 tbsp brewers yeast or wheat-germ
½ cup asparagus, cooked or raw, cut into ½ inch long pieces
1 clove garlic, crushed (optional)
1 tsp lemon juice

what to do
1. Place the salmon in a 350°F oven on a greased baking sheet and cook for about 15 minutes until just cooked through.
2. Meanwhile, cook the wild rice according to the package directions until tender and soft. All the water should be absorbed.
3. Combine all the ingredients in a large mixing bowl and stir thoroughly.
4. Store in a refrigerator for 2 to 3 days and serve portions appropriate for your pet, either as a stand alone meal or as an accompaniment to her usual food.

The homeopathic remedy Thuja is excellent for helping to address adverse vaccine reactions. Some holistic vets recommend a dose prior to vaccination; otherwise you can just give it for a few days afterwards. Consult your holistic vet for a dosage recommendation. Always try to space out vaccines and really think about which immunizations your pet needs. Many pets in the United States are seriously over-vaccinated and this can take a huge toll in the immune system and in some cases, pre-dispose a pet to diseases like cancer. Your vet can help you choose which vaccines are needed based on the risk factors of your geographical location and lifestyle.

cancer diet: turkey & yams

This simple diet contains only fresh, wholesome ingredients with fewer carbohydrates and an emphasis on protein. Since cancers have been found to grow on a high carbohydrate diet, it's important to keep carbohydrates to a minimum and feed lots of extra protein when the disease has been diagnosed.

ingredients
3 cups of organic turkey, ground or diced
½ cup of organic yams
½ cup of organic live culture plain yogurt
½ cup organic green beans

what to do
1. Sauté the turkey until cooked through.
2. Combine all the ingredients in a large mixing bowl and stir thoroughly.
3. Store in a refrigerator for 2 to 3 days and serve portions appropriate for your pet, either as a stand alone meal or as an accompaniment to their usual food.

Many vets recommend a cooked diet for pets with a compromised immune system such as those who are battling cancer because unlike a healthy pet with a robust immune system, they may not be able to tolerate any trace amounts of bacteria that may be present.

cancer diet: sardines & sweet potatoes

This simple diet contains only fresh, wholesome ingredients with fewer carbohydrates and an emphasis on protein. Since cancers have been found to grow on a high carbohydrate diet, it's important to keep carbohydrates to a minimum and feed lots of extra protein when the disease has been diagnosed.

ingredients
3 cups of canned sardines in water
½ cup organic sweet potatoes
½ cup cottage cheese
½ cup organic leafy greens, finely chopped
1 cup The Honest Kitchen Embark™ dehydrated dog food
1 cup filtered water
4 tsp organic flaxseed oil

what to do
1. Hydrate the Embark™ with the warm water in a large bowl.
2. Stir in the remaining ingredients carefully with a wooden spoon, trying not to break up the sardines too much.
3. Store the mixture in a refrigerator for 2 to 3 days and serve portions appropriate for your pet, either as a stand alone meal or as an accompaniment to her usual food.
4. If you wish, you can moisten and loosen the food a little before serving, by simply adding in some additional warm water and stirring gently.

itchy skin fish mush

This grain-free recipe uses Dover sole, which is a 'novel' protein for many pets who may be itchy from consuming more common proteins like lamb or chicken.

ingredients
2 cups Dover sole or other white fish
1 cup sweet potatoes
3 tbsp flaxseed or evening primrose oil
2 lugs of olive oil
2 tablespoons fresh dandelion or parsley leaves, chopped (optional)

what to do
1. Peel and dice the sweet potatoes and boil in water until they are very soft and tender.
2. Meanwhile, lightly sauté the sole in a pan with some olive oil (you can also serve the sole raw if you prefer).
3. Combine the sole and sweet potatoes in a large mixing bowl and add in the flaxseed or evening primrose oil.
4. Stir in the dandelion and serve a portion appropriate for your pet's size.

If your pet suffers with chronic itching and scratching all year round, the cause could well be a food sensitivity. Try completely eliminating grain from his or her diet for a few weeks (remember this also includes grain-based treats!) and see if there is any improvement.

Dandelion is a cleansing herb that can help remove toxins from your pet's system, thus helping to relieve itchiness in many cases. It's also an exceedingly rich source of vitamins A, C, K, B complex and D as well as potassium, iron and manganese.

If your pet's itchiness is strictly seasonal, check carefully for fleas. Some pets also suffer from contact allergies in the warmer months but a healthy, whole-food diet can go a long way to building up the immune system and making the effects less troublesome for your pet.

g♥odness
in the raw

The recipes in this section are great for cats and dogs, but not for people since they contain raw meats. I don't recommend feeding raw food combined with kibble because the two will be digested at different rates and this can lead to possible health concerns.

It's fine to use bones in these recipes because they are uncooked but take care to grind the bone to a size that is easily digestible for your pet, and introduce gradually to prevent any rapid gobbling that could present a health hazard. You should also discuss the suitability of raw meals for your particular pet, with your holistic veterinarian.

Take great care to prepare raw foods for your pet very carefully. Thoroughly clean surfaces and utensils and store your ingredients properly just as you would for the foods you eat yourself, so that bacteria are less likely to reproduce.

I don't typically recommend large raw bones unless you're a very experienced raw feeder and your dog is used to them, because in some cases they can still cause problems sometimes. As raw food diets have gained popularity, the incidence of veterinary procedures to remove bones from the GI tract has also increased. When swallowed, whole raw bones or bone shards can obstruct the intestines, cause constipation, lodge in the roof of the mouth and break the teeth in extreme cases. For this reason, a high powered food grinder that is capable of pulverizing the bones to a manageable size can be a really great investment if you'd like to start making lots of your pets meals, yourself.

One final word of caution: do not re-freeze any recipes that are made with previously frozen raw ingredients because this can result in excessive levels of harmful bacteria developing.

beef liver & greens

ingredients
3 cups fresh raw, organic beef liver
1 cup fresh spinach
¼ cup fresh broccoli
¼ cup fresh kale
1 handful fresh parsley
1 clove raw garlic
2 good lugs of extra virgin olive oil

what to do
1. Dice the beef liver with a sharp knife, into bite-sized pieces appropriate for your pet and set aside in a large bowl.
2. Roughly chop the green vegetables and parsley.
3. Add them to the bowl with the beef.
4. Crush the garlic and add to the other ingredients.
5. Mix in the olive oil.
6. Stir all the ingredients thoroughly.
7. Serve in a portion appropriate for your pet.
8. This recipe will store for up to 2 days in a refrigerator.

It's important to buy organic beef liver if you can. One of the liver's roles in the body is to process medications and toxins that the meat-producing animal is exposed to. Feeding liver from an animal that has been raised organically means there was less exposure to toxins and therefore less of these toxins remain in the liver itself.

chicken liver puree

This is a bright orange and yellow combination that's really nourishing and is ideal for a pet who needs a little pepping up!

ingredients

2 cups fresh raw chicken livers (organic if possible)
⅓ cup raw carrots, roughly chopped
1 cup sweet potato, peeled and roughly chopped
1 peach or nectarine, pit removed
4 fresh basil leaves

what to do

1. Add all the ingredients to a food processor or blender and process on until they are chopped and mixed to your pet's desired consistency.
2. You can use less of the vegetables and fruits for cats, if you wish.
3. You can store this recipe for up to 2 days in a refrigerator.

Sweet potatoes are really useful for tummy troubles. They calm the GI tract and help to combat both diarrhea and constipation, with their naturally high fiber content. They are also a great source of beta carotene. If your pet is very sensitive, it's fine to steam the sweet potatoes for this recipe to make them a little more easily digestible, if you wish.

venison mush

This colorful blend is laden with amino acids, antioxidants, fiber and healthy fats.

ingredients

3 cups venison, diced into bite-sized pieces appropriate for your pet
½ cup fresh or frozen papaya dices
½ cup fresh or frozen peas
(or substitute mange-tout or sugar-snap peas, roughly chopped)
¼ cup plain full-fat yogurt
¼ cup ground flaxseed meal
2 tbsp apple cider vinegar
2 free range eggs

what to do

1. Combine all the ingredients in a large mixing bowl and stir thoroughly.
2. Store in a covered container in a refrigerator for up to 2 days.
3. Serve in size-appropriate portions for your pet.

Holistic veterinarians recommend Apple Cider Vinegar for a wealth of different ailments in cats and dogs, including allergies, arthritis, hot spots, loss of appetite and ear infections. It also helps to establish correct pH balance within the body.

turkey medley

This is a simple combination that contains plenty of vitamin A.
The cottage cheese is a nice balance to the other flavors.

ingredients

3 cups ground raw turkey or turkey necks
¼ cup fresh small broccoli florets
¼ cup fresh string beans
⅓ cup fresh mango
2 free range eggs
½ cup cottage cheese

what to do

1. Chop the broccoli and green beans finely and set aside in a large bowl.
2. Then mash up the mango flesh with a fork and add to the bowl.
3. Beat the eggs using a whisk or fork. Mix the turkey, eggs and cottage cheese into the bowl.
4. Stir thoroughly so that all the ingredients are evenly combined.
5. Combine all the ingredients in a large mixing bowl and stir thoroughly.
6. Store in a covered container in a refrigerator for up to 2 days.
7. Serve in size-appropriate portions for your pet.

Mangoes contain a number of vitamins and antioxidants that are believed to help in the prevention of cancer. Naturopaths also recommend mango to help combat acidity and poor digestion. Mango is a rich source of beta-carotene, vitamin E and selenium which protect against a number of ailments including heart disease.

lamb & garden vegetables

This simple combination makes a delicious raw topping to your pet's usual food. The mix does get a little mushy if stored for too long, so this recipe is best used within a day or two.

ingredients

3 cups ground raw lamb or lamb and bones
½ cup chopped raw kale
¼ cup fresh broccoli florets, finely chopped
½ cup plain cottage cheese
1 banana, roughly chopped

what to do

1. Combine all ingredients in a bowl and stir thoroughly.
2. Store in a refrigerator and serve as required depending on your pet's size and appetite.

Broccoli is rich in vitamin C, vitamin A and manganese. It's also rich in many phyto-nutrients that are thought to be protective against many types of cancer.

mediterranean chicken

The healthy Mediterranean diet contains lots of fresh healthy vegetables and fruits including olives and tomatoes, as well as, olive oil and basil. Mediterranean diets contain a moderate amount of fish and poultry but little red meat as a general rule.

ingredients
3 cups ground chicken necks and wings or chicken meat
1 tomato, finely chopped
4 tbsp olive oil
½ cup romaine lettuce, roughly chopped
2 tbsp chopped basil
⅓ cup plain yogurt

what to do
1. Combine all ingredients in a bowl and stir thoroughly.
2. Store in a refrigerator and serve as required depending on your pet's size and appetite.

Olive oil is rich in antioxidants and mono-unsaturated fats. Tomatoes contain Lycopene and vitamin C.

duck & plums

Just use the main bulb of the fennel for this recipe – remove the darker green part of the stalk and the tough thick part of the root at the bottom.

ingredients

3 cups raw duck meat or ground meat and bones
4 plums, pitted
1 cup raw fennel, finely chopped
2 tbsp olive oil
½ cup grated carrots
½ cup grated cucumber

what to do

1. Combine all the ingredients in a large mixing bowl and stir thoroughly.
2. Store in a covered container in a refrigerator for up to 2 days.
3. Serve in size-appropriate portions for your pet.

According to traditional Chinese medicine, plums are a cooling food with an affinity for the stomach and liver. Plums clear liver heat and are used in therapies for liver disease, in traditional Chinese medicine practices. Take care to ensure all stones are removed from the plums as they can represent a choking hazard if swallowed.

turkey & tropical fruits

You could also include, or substitute other tropical fruits like papayas and pineapple in this recipe, as well as, some unrefined coconut oil to increase the fat content, if you'd like.

ingredients

3 cups ground raw turkey or ground turkey and bones
1 banana, sliced
1 mango, soft flesh only, roughly chopped
1 cup kale, roughly chopped
¼ cup coconut milk

what to do

1. Combine all the ingredients in a large mixing bowl and stir thoroughly.
2. Store in a covered container in a refrigerator for up to 2 days.
3. Serve in size-appropriate portions for your pet.

In traditional Chinese medicine, banana is a cooling food that has an affinity for the stomach and large intestine. It also promotes body fluids and is useful for dry throat and thirst, as well as constipation.

venison & yams

If your pet isn't keen on the tart taste of berries, other fruits like banana or melon would be good substitutes as they have a much milder taste. They can be mashed up for smaller pets.

ingredients

3 cups venison meat or ground meaty bones
1 cup raw grated yams
½ cup fresh or frozen blueberries
1½ cups romaine lettuce, roughly chopped
½ cup kefir or cottage cheese

what to do

1. Combine the meat and grated yams in a bowl and stir thoroughly.
2. Gently fold in the romaine and blueberries.
3. Add the cottage cheese or kefir as a topping or stir in to coat the other ingredients if you prefer.
4. Store in a refrigerator and serve as required in portions appropriate for your pet; you can alternate with his regular meals or feed this for each meal until it's all gone.

According to the principles of traditional Chinese medicine, Venison is a warming food which tonifies Yang Qi. Studies show that animals fed blueberries over a prolonged period of time, show fewer age-related motor changes than animals who have no blueberries included in their diets.

beef & cranberries

You could also use fresh cranberries, or any other dried or fresh berries
(but not grapes or raisins) in this recipe, if you wish.

ingredients

3 cups ground beef
⅔ cups dried unsweetened cranberries
2 free range eggs
3 tbsp safflower oil
½ cup cottage cheese
½ cup fresh watercress, chopped

what to do

1. Combine the beef, cranberries, oil and eggs in a bowl and stir thoroughly.
2. Gently fold in the cottage cheese and watercress so everything is thoroughly combined.
3. Store in a refrigerator and serve as required in portions appropriate for the size of your pet.

Cranberries contain a substance that helps to prevent the adhesion of bacteria to the bladder walls, and are therefore supportive for urinary tract health. Adding pure, unsweetened cranberry juice to your pet's food or drinking water is also beneficial for those who are prone to urinary tract infections.

juicing for pets

Juicing is an easy way to meet your daily requirements of fruits and vegetables, and to consume some raw foods that are easy to digest. It's also a great thing to share with your pet and allow him or her to reap the benefits. Here are some fruits and vegetables that are great for juicing, and some of the benefits associated with them according to the principles of traditional Chinese medicine.

apples
Ease thirst, reduce fever, and ease dry, hot lungs (green apples also cleanse the liver).

beets
Purify the blood, alleviate constipation and aid the liver.

carrots
Support the lungs and spleen, pancreas and liver.

celery
Heals wounds, alleviates constipation and reduces liver congestion.

cucumber
Supports the stomach and bladder, relieves edema and helps with difficult urination.

peaches
Promote blood circulation and lubricate the intestines.

pineapple
Aids in digestion of starches and protein, relieves chronic lung congestion and has anti-inflammatory properties.

squash
Supports the spleen and stomach, heals inflammation and relieves pain.

yam
Tonifies the lungs, spleen and kidneys. Helpful for diarrhea and coughs.

watermelon
Supports the stomach, heart and bladder. Clears heat, induces urination and relieves thirst.

index

almonds, almond meal, almond butter
17   cooling summer duck parfait
18   salmon & peach cooler
31   nutty pumpkin rounds
34   almond butter poppers
35   holiday noshers
39   banana pupcakes

alfalfa
87   bone & joint support

apple cider vinegar
67   fruity chicken salad
97   venison mush

applesauce, unsweetened
27   healthy autumn brownies
35   holiday noshers

liver loaf
47   valentines liver nibbles

apricots
15   sardine & apricot mush

asparagus
89   immune support

bananas
39   banana pupcakes
88   stress less
99   lamb & garden vegetables
102 turkey & tropical fruits

basil
18   salmon & peach cooler
47   valentines liver nibbles
55   canine quiche
96   chicken liver puree
100 mediterranean chicken

bay leaf
60   potato, kale & celery root soup

beans (string, green)
56   cream sole with summer garden vegetables
83   diabetes – Verve™
90   cancer diet: turkey & jams
98   turkey medley

beef, ground; beef stew meat; beef liver
34   almond butter poppers
37   liver loaf
43   gluten-free halloween bonbons
45   summer savories
53   nourishing fall stew
55   canine quiche
65   mix' match meat stew
81   fleas
83   diabetes – Verve™
95   beef liver & greens
104 beef & cranberries

bell pepper
68   ostrich burgers
70   zucchini chicken & rice casserole

bison
69   bison meatballs
84   sensitive tummies exotic blend

blueberries
25   antioxidant-rich blueberry muffins
35   holiday noshers
56   cream sole with summer garden vegetables
103 venison & yams

bread crumbs
69   bison meatballs

broccoli
65   mix' match meat stew
95   beef liver & greens
98   turkey medley
99   lamb & garden vegetables

buckwheat, buckwheat flour
19   warming buckwheat cream
43   gluten-free halloween bonbons

butter
22   pinch of parsley
60   potato, kale & celery root soup

butternut squash
40   butternut bites
53   nourishing fall stew

carrots
53   nourishing fall stew
56   cream sole with summer garden vegetables
57   hearty winter stew
65   mix' match meat stew
70   zucchini chicken & rice casserole
96   chicken liver puree
101 duck & plums

catnip
78   divine feline scramble

cayenne pepper
86   flexibility fish medley
87   bone & joint support

celery
53   nourishing fall stew
60   potato, kale & celery root soup
67   fruity chicken salad

cheese
27   healthy autumn brownies
29   dream drops
45   summer savories
50   turkey & cranberry savories
55   canine quiche
69   bison meatballs
70   zucchini chicken & rice casserole
75   feline valentine savories
103 venison & yams

cherries
13   springtime topper

chamomile tea
88   stress less

**chicken, ground; chicken organs;
chicken liver; chicken stock**
16   chicken with yam & coconut milk puree
47   valentines liver nibbles
49   simple roasted organs
55   canine quiche
57   hearty winter stew
60   potato, kale & celery root soup
65   mix' match meat stew
67   fruity chicken salad
70   zucchini chicken & rice casserole
73   prowlmelet

77   liver cake for cats
83   diabetes – Verve™
87   bone & joint support
96   chicken liver puree
100 mediterranean chicken

cilantro
61   coconutty turkey soup
69   bison meatballs

cinnamon
69   bison meatballs

coconut milk
16   chicken with yam & coconut milk puree
61   coconutty turkey soup
102 turkey & tropical fruits

cottage cheese
21   sardine salad
56   cream sole with summer garden vegetables
91   cancer diet: sardines & sweet potatoes
98   turkey medley
99   lamb & garden vegetables
103 venison & yams
104 beef & cranberries

cranberries
34   almond butter poppers
40   butternut bites
44   pilgrim patties
47   valentines liver nibbles
50   turkey & cranberry savories
73   prowlmelet
104 beef & cranberries

cucumber
17   cooling summer duck parfait
18   salmon & peach cooler
101 duck & plums

dandelion greens
82   diabetes – Keen™
92   itchy skin fish mush

dill
64   salmon saves the day

duck
17   cooling summer duck parfait
101 duck & plums

index

eggs
25   antioxidant-rich blueberry muffins
28   green force & ham treats
29   dream drops
33   puppalicious doggie birthday cake
37   liver loaf
39   banana pupcakes
41   chicken & garlic treats
43   gluten-free halloween bonbons
44   pilgrim patties
45   summer savories
47   valentines liver nibbles
50   turkey & cranberry savories
55   canine quiche
63   simple lamb bake
69   bison meatballs
73   prowlmelet
75   feline valentine savories
77   liver cake for cats
78   divine feline scramble
81   fleas
97   venison mush
98   turkey medley
104   beef & cranberries

Embark™ dog food
31   nutty pumpkin rounds
39   banana pupcakes
44   pilgrim patties
91   cancer diet: sardines & sweet potatoes

fava beans
13   springtime topper

fennel
13   springtime topper
59   healthy fish & sweet potato bake
101   duck & plums

flax (ground or oil)
25   antioxidant-rich blueberry muffins
34   almond butter poppers
37   liver loaf
97   venison mush

Force™ dog food
27   healthy autumn brownies
33   a puppalicious doggie birthday cake
28   green Force™ & ham treats
43   gluten-free halloween bonbons

garlic
37   liver loaf
41   chicken & garlic treats
47   valentines liver nibbles
49   simple roasted organs
53   nourishing fall stew
57   hearty winter stew
59   healthy fish & sweet potato bake
60   potato, kale & celery root soup
68   ostrich burgers
69   bison meatballs
70   zucchini chicken & rice casserole
81   fleas
89   immune support
95   beef liver & greens

ginger
61   coconutty turkey soup

green beans
21   sardine salad
50   turkey & cranberry savories
82   diabetes – Keen™

ham
27   healthy autumn brownies
28   green Force™ & ham treats
29   dream drops

honey
17   cooling summer duck parfait
18   salmon & peach cooler
33   a puppalicious doggie birthday cake
39   banana pupcakes
40   butternut bites

Ice Pups™ treat mix
33   a puppalicious doggie birthday cake

kale

57 hearty winter stew
60 potato, kale & celery root soup
91 cancer diet: sardines & sweet potatoes
95 beef liver & greens
99 lamb & garden vegetables
102 turkey & tropical fruits

Keen™ dog food

45 summer savories
50 turkey & cranberry savories
82 diabetes – Keen™

kefir

55 canine quiche

kelp

25 antioxidant-rich blueberry muffins
37 liver loaf
41 chicken & garlic treats
81 fleas

lamb

57 hearty winter stew
63 simple lamb bake
99 lamb & garden vegetables

lemon juice

61 coconutty turkey soup
89 immune support

lettuce

88 stress less
100 mediterranean chicken
103 venison & yams

mango

98 turkey medley
102 turkey & tropical fruits

melon

21 sardine salad
67 fruity chicken salad

milk

34 almond butter poppers
60 potato, kale & celery root soup

millet

15 sardine & apricot mush
88 stress less

nectarine

96 chicken liver puree

oats, oat flour, oatmeal

28 green Force™ & ham treats
34 almond butter poppers
35 holiday noshers
40 butternut bites
77 liver cake for cats
86 flexibility fish medley
88 stress less

oil (flax, salmon or safflower)

82 diabetes – Keen™
83 diabetes – Verve™
86 flexibility fish medley
87 bone & joint support
91 cancer diet: sardines & sweet potatoes
92 itchy skin fish mush
104 beef & cranberries

olive oil

16 chicken with yam & coconut milk puree
17 cooling summer duck parfait
18 salmon & peach cooler
19 warming buckwheat cream
25 antioxidant-rich blueberry muffins
47 valentines liver nibbles
49 simple roasted organs
53 nourishing fall stew
55 canine quiche
57 hearty winter stew
59 healthy fish & sweet potato bake
60 potato, kale & celery root soup
64 salmon saves the day
68 ostrich burgers
70 zucchini chicken & rice casserole
92 itchy skin fish mush
95 beef liver & greens
100 mediterranean chicken
101 duck & plums

ostrich

68 ostrich burgers

index

papaya
17   cooling summer duck parfait
84   sensitive tummies exotic blend
97   venison mush

parsnips
27   healthy autumn brownies

parsley
17   cooling summer duck parfait
22   a pinch of parsley
44   pilgrim patties
56   creamy sole with summer garden vegetables
78   divine feline scramble
83   diabetes – Verve™
92   itchy skin fish mush
95   beef liver & greens

peaches
67   fruity chicken salad

peas
97   venison mush

pineapple juice
67   fruity chicken salad

plums
101 duck & plums

potatoes – white or yukon
60   potato, kale & celery root soup
96   chicken liver puree

Preference™ dog food
57   hearty winter stew
63   simple lamb bake

Prowl™ cat food
73   prowlmelet
75   feline valentine savories
78   divine feline scramble

pumpkin
15   sardine & apricot mush
31   nutty pumpkin rounds
43   gluten-free halloween bonbons
44   pilgrim patties
77   liver cake for cats

quinoa
43   gluten-free halloween bonbons
47   valentines liver nibbles
82   diabetes – Keen™
87   bone & joint support

rice
70   zucchini chicken & rice casserole
89   immune support

rosemary
27   healthy autumn brownies
49   simple roasted organs
70   zucchini chicken & rice casserole

salmon
18   salmon & peach cooler
64   salmon saves the day
86   flexibility fish medley
89   immune support

sardines
15   sardine & apricot mush
21   sardine salad
91   cancer diet: sardines & sweet potatoes

Smooches™ or Nuzzles™
33   a puppalicious doggie birthday cake

sole
56   creamy sole with summer garden vegetables
59   healthy fish & sweet potato bake
92   itchy skin fish mush

sour cream
67   fruity chicken salad

spinach
17   cooling summer duck parfait
55   canine quiche
61   coconutty turkey soup
95   beef liver & greens

spirulina
15   sardine & apricot mush
81   fleas

squash
65   mix' match meat stew

sweet potatoes
22   a pinch of parsley
27   healthy autumn brownies
50   turkey & cranberry savories
57   hearty winter stew
59   healthy fish & sweet potato bake
63   simple lamb bake
84   sensitive tummies exotic blend
85   sensitive tummies simple bake (or not)
91   cancer diet: sardines & sweet potatoes
92   itchy skin fish mush

Thrive™ dog food
29   dream drops
35   holiday noshers
41   chicken & garlic treats

tomatoes
53   nourishing fall stew
70   zucchini chicken & rice casserole
100 mediterranean chicken

turkey
44   pilgrim patties
44   turkey & cranberry savories
61   coconutty turkey soup
65   mix' match meat stew
75   feline valentine savories
78   divine feline scramble
82   diabetes – Keen™
85   sensitive tummies simple bake (or not)
88   stress less
90   cancer diet: turkey & yams
98   turkey medley
102 turkey & tropical fruits

turnip
53   nourishing fall stew

vegetable oil
77   liver cake for cats

venison
84   sensitive tummies exotic blend
97   venison mush
103 venison & yams

Verve™ dog food
34   almond butter poppers
83   diabetes – Verve™
81   fleas

watercress
64   salmon saves the day
104 beef & cranberries

wheatgerm
25   antioxidant-rich blueberry muffins

wheatgrass
78   divine feline scramble

yams
16   chicken with yam & coconut milk puree
83   diabetes – Verve™
90   cancer diet: turkey & yams
103 venison & yams

yeast
25   antioxidant-rich blueberry muffins
37   liver loaf
40   butternut bites
41   chicken & garlic treats
77   liver cake for cats
81   fleas
88   stress less
89   immune support

yogurt
13   springtime topper
15   sardine & apricot mush
18   salmon & peach cooler
25   antioxidant-rich blueberry muffins
28   green Force™ & ham treats
33   a puppalicious doggie birthday cake
34   almond butter poppers
39   banana pupcakes
56   creamy sole with summer garden vegetables
67   fruity chicken salad
78   divine feline scramble
84   sensitive tummies exotic blend
89   immune support
90   cancer diet: turkey & yams
97   venison mush
100 mediterranean chicken

zucchini
45   summer savories
56   creamy sole with summer garden vegetables
65   mix' match meat stew
70   zucchini chicken & rice casserole